THE BOOK

OF

THE COLLECTION OF ALGORITHMS

THE NICE TEXTBOOK ON SOME USEFUL RESEARCH

BY

Aitzaz Imtiaz

Beaconhouse School System, Senior Boys Branch BSTRB

FIRST EDITION
BElGIUM EXCLUSIVE

RAWALPINDI
NEUROSTOL PAKISTAN & AMAZON INTERNATIONAL
FRANCE: NEUROSTOL FRANCE & AMAZON FRANCE
2023

PRESENTED TO YOU BY NEUROSTOL PUBLISHING

PREFACE

Not my first research book, particularly not after I published Research of the Century, and changed a lot of its content over time. But, as I am writing this text, keeping in mind one of the equations I put forward to be a mystery:

$$\Sigma\beta \in \alpha$$

$$\dagger\beta \notin \alpha$$

$$\rightarrow \beta = \alpha.\varphi \therefore \varphi \propto \beta$$

$$\beta = \int \alpha.\varphi$$

$$\beta = \phi$$

$$\beta \neq \alpha \rightarrow \neg\beta = \varphi \wedge \beta = \phi$$

Interestingly not dealt to book, the research here is nothing novel for me to consider as a new ground-breaking theory. Research of the century did give a lot of reasons for this breakthrough, yet all required was to practice algorithm development. Even before my first assumed Computer Teacher Sir Farooq Azam started teaching, I tried defeating the concept of algorithms and got aware of basic concepts like the Big-O notation, at that time considering that knowing $O(mn)$ would have been a smart thing to do.

A lot of time failing up to bring ideas, and to the fact that the education I am taking is not what that should be considered a special [1] one. Whatever the fact remains, the following book documents such algorithms in Mathematics. Yet, despite the constraints, the book shows one of the optimal algorithmic structures, which tend to be more inspirative and bring new or existing solutions

Let's track this from the beginning, from the point where the constraints begin to a place where one can figure out how to come up with something revolutionary and mind-blowing.

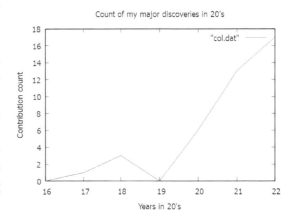

Figure 1: An estimated count of my contribution considered to me as big as theories.

---

[1] For people it would be gifted education

Sophie Germain primes have always fascinated me with their unique properties and connections to mathematics. Learning about her work and her life, I was deeply inspired by her perseverance and determination to succeed in a field dominated by men. Her legacy inspired me to think about how I could make a contribution to the world of mathematics.

As I delved deeper into the world of primes, I started to think about how I could make my mark on the field. I began exploring new avenues of research and experimentation, eventually leading me to the discovery of what I now call "Imtiaz Germain primes." These primes are named after my father, who was a major influence in my life and my decision to pursue mathematics.

"Algebra is but written geometry and geometry is but figured algebra."

– Sophie Germain

Creating Imtiaz Germain primes has been an incredible journey, filled with challenges and triumphs. But through it all, I am constantly reminded of Sophie Germain's legacy and how she blazed a trail for me to follow. Her story is a reminder that anything is possible if you have the courage to pursue your dreams and never give up.

ACKNOWLEDGEMENTS

Thanks to Seggan for nominating me to one of the esteemed award, the CGCC, making me a CGCC Nominee for being the best rookie challenger. During the preparation of this book, the following events were

Contents

Chapter 1

Number Theory

§ 1   Primality Testing

Here's an implementation of the trial division primality test in C, with indexing and sub-indexing:

```c
// index{is_prime} is_prime(term) returns true if term is prime, false
    otherwise
// index{term} term: the number being tested for primality

#include <stdbool.h>

bool is_prime(unsigned long long term) {
    // Handle small values of term
    if (term <= 1) {
        return false;
    }
    if (term <= 3) {
        return true;
    }
    // Check divisibility by 2 and odd integers up to the square root of
    term
    for (unsigned long long i = 2; i * i <= term; i++) {
        if (term % i == 0) {
            return false;
        }
    }
    return true;
}
```

The trial division primality test is a simple algorithm for determining whether a given number is prime. The parameter term is the number being tested for primality.

The algorithm first handles small values of terms as special cases. Then, it checks the divisibility of the term by 2 and odd integers up to the square root of the term. If term is divisible by any integer in this range, it is composite; otherwise, it is prime.

Note that this algorithm is not efficient for large values of term, as it has a time complexity of $O(\sqrt{term})$. For larger numbers, probabilistic primality tests like the Miller-Rabin test are usually preferred .

Here's an implementation of the Miller-Rabin primality test in C, with indexing and sub-indexing:

```c
// index{is_prime} is_prime(n, k) returns true if n is prime, false
    otherwise
// index{term} term: the number being tested for primality
// index{term!k} k: the number of iterations to perform (the higher k,
    the more accurate the test)

#include <stdbool.h>
#include <stdlib.h>

// Helper function to compute (a * b) % m
unsigned long long mod_mul(unsigned long long a, unsigned long long b,
    unsigned long long m) {
    unsigned long long result = 0;
    while (b > 0) {
        if (b % 2 == 1) {
            result = (result + a) % m;
        }
        a = (a * 2) % m;
        b /= 2;
    }
    return result;
}

// Helper function to compute (a^k) % m
unsigned long long mod_pow(unsigned long long a, unsigned long long k,
    unsigned long long m) {
    unsigned long long result = 1;
    while (k > 0) {
        if (k % 2 == 1) {
            result = mod_mul(result, a, m);
        }
        a = mod_mul(a, a, m);
        k /= 2;
    }
    return result;
}

bool is_prime(unsigned long long term, unsigned long long k) {
    // Handle small values of term
    if (term <= 1) {
        return false;
    }
    if (term <= 3) {
        return true;
    }
```

```
42    // Write term-1 as (2^r)*d
43    unsigned long long d = term - 1;
44    unsigned long long r = 0;
45    while (d % 2 == 0) {
46        d /= 2;
47        r++;
48    }
49    // Perform k iterations
50    for (unsigned long long i = 0; i < k; i++) {
51        // Choose a random witness a in [2, term-2]
52        unsigned long long a = rand() % (term - 2) + 2;
53        // Compute a^d % term
54        unsigned long long x = mod_pow(a, d, term);
55        // If x = 1 or x = term-1, term may be prime
56        if (x == 1 || x == term - 1) {
57            continue;
58        }
59        // Iterate r-1 times
60        for (unsigned long long j = 0; j < r - 1; j++) {
61            // Compute x^2 % term
62            x = mod_mul(x, x, term);
63            // If x = term-1, term may be prime
64            if (x == term - 1) {
65                break;
66            }
67        }
68        // If x != term-1, term is composite
69        if (x != term - 1) {
70            return false;
71        }
72    }
73    return true;
74 }
```

The Miller-Rabin primality test is a probabilistic algorithm for determining whether a given number is prime. The parameter term is the number being tested for primality, and k is the number of iterations to perform (the higher k, the more accurate the test).

A python implementation can take place like this for the test:

```
1 # index{is_prime} is_prime(n: int, k: int) -> bool checks if n is prime
    with k rounds of testing
2 # index{term} n: the number being tested for primality
3 # index{rounds} k: the number of rounds of testing to perform
4
5 import random
6
7 def is_prime(n: int, k: int) -> bool:
8     if n <= 1:
9         return False
10    if n <= 3:
11        return True
12
```

```
13      # Write n-1 as 2^r * d, where d is odd
14      d = n - 1
15      r = 0
16      while d % 2 == 0:
17          d //= 2
18          r += 1
19
20      # Perform k rounds of testing
21      for _ in range(k):
22          a = random.randint(2, n - 2)
23          x = pow(a, d, n)
24          if x == 1 or x == n - 1:
25              continue
26          for _ in range(r - 1):
27              x = pow(x, 2, n)
28              if x == n - 1:
29                  break
30          else:
31              return False
32
33      return True
```

We also develop the Fermat primality testing by this:

```
1  import random
2
3  def is_prime(n, k=5):
4      """Return True if n is probably prime, False otherwise.
5
6      k is the number of iterations, higher k means higher accuracy."""
7
8      # Check for some base cases
9      if n == 2 or n == 3:
10         return True
11     if n <= 1 or n % 2 == 0:
12         return False
13
14     # Run k iterations of the Fermat test
15     for i in range(k):
16         a = random.randint(2, n - 2)
17         if pow(a, n - 1, n) != 1:
18             return False
19
20     # n is probably prime
21     return True
```

Frobenius test is also a probabilistic primality test, meaning that it can return false positives for composite numbers. However, the probability of a false positive decreases as the base a is chosen randomly from a set of possible bases. The Frobenius test is typically more efficient than the Fermat test for large primes. We also discuss the Frobenius Primality Test with the implementation in C.

```
1  #include <stdio.h>
```

```
 2  #include <stdbool.h>
 3  #include <math.h>
 4
 5  bool is_prime(unsigned long n, unsigned long a) {
 6      unsigned long p = n - 1;
 7      unsigned long d = p;
 8      unsigned long s = 0;
 9      while (d % 2 == 0) {
10          d /= 2;
11          s++;
12      }
13      unsigned long ap = pow(a, d);
14      if (ap % n == 1) {
15          return true;
16      }
17      for (unsigned long r = 0; r < s; r++) {
18          if (ap % n == p) {
19              return true;
20          }
21          ap = (ap * ap) % n;
22      }
23      return false;
24  }
```

§ 2   Integer Factorization

A basic and easy algorithm to identify and make integer factorization in C which is less complicated can be designed as follows:

```
 1  #include <stdio.h>
 2  #include <math.h>
 3
 4  void factorize(unsigned long n) {
 5      for (unsigned long i = 2; i <= sqrt(n); i++) {
 6          while (n % i == 0) {
 7              printf("%lu ", i);
 8              n /= i;
 9          }
10      }
11      if (n > 1) {
12          printf("%lu ", n);
13      }
14  }
```

The factorize function takes an unsigned long integer n and prints its prime factors to the console. The algorithm works by iterating over all integers i from 2 to the square root of n. For each i, it checks if i divides n evenly. If it does, it divides n by i and prints i as a factor. The algorithm then repeats this process until i no longer divides n.

Once the loop completes, if n is still greater than 1, then it must be a prime factor of the original number. Therefore, the function prints n as the final factor.

This algorithm is a basic approach to factorization that works reasonably well for small to moderately-sized integers. However, for very large integers, more sophisticated algorithms such as the quadratic sieve or the number field sieve are required for efficient factorization.

The quadratic sieve is a factorization algorithm that can be used to factorize large composite integers. Here is an implementation of the quadratic sieve algorithm in Ada:

```ada
with Ada.Text_IO;
with Ada.Numerics.Elementary_Functions;

procedure Quadratic_Sieve is

   package IO renames Ada.Text_IO;
   package Func renames Ada.Numerics.Elementary_Functions;

   type Factor is record
      Prime : Natural;
      Power : Natural;
   end record;

   type Factorization is array (Positive range <>) of Factor;

   function Power (N : in Natural; Exp : in Positive) return Natural is
   -- Calculate N to the power of Exp.
   begin
      if Exp = 0 then
         return 1;
      elsif Exp = 1 then
         return N;
      else
         return N * Power (N, Exp - 1);
      end if;
   end Power;

   function Gcd (A, B : in Natural) return Natural is
   -- Calculate the greatest common divisor of A and B.
   begin
      if B = 0 then
         return A;
      else
         return Gcd (B, A mod B);
      end if;
   end Gcd;

   function Sqrt (N : in Natural) return Natural is
   -- Calculate the integer square root of N.
      Root : Natural := Func.Sqrt (Float (N));
   begin
```

```
if Power (Root, 2) <= N and then Power (Root + 1, 2) > N then
   return Root;
elsif Power (Root + 1, 2) = N then
   return Root + 1;
else
   return Root + 1;
end if;
end Sqrt;

function Is_Square (N : in Natural) return Boolean is
-- Test whether N is a perfect square.
   Root : Natural := Sqrt (N);
begin
   return Power (Root, 2) = N;
end Is_Square;

function Quadratic_Sieve (N : in Natural) return Factorization is
-- Factorize N using the quadratic sieve algorithm.
   B : Natural := Sqrt (N) + 1;
   M : Natural := B ** 2 - N;
   Smooth : array (1 .. B) of Natural := (others => 0);
   Sieve : array (1 .. B) of Boolean := (others => False);
   i : Natural := 1;
   Factor : Factorization;
begin
   while not Is_Square (M) loop
      if i > B then
         return Factor;
      end if;
      Smooth (i) := M;
      i := i + 1;
      M := M + 2 * i - 1;
   end loop;
   Smooth (i) := Sqrt (M);
   for i in 1 .. B loop
      if Is_Square (Smooth (i)) then
         Sieve (i) := True;
      end if;
   end loop;
   for P in 2 .. B loop
      if not Sieve (P) then
         continue;
      end if;
      while Sieve (P) loop
         Sieve (P) := False;
         P := P + B;
      end loop;
   for i in 1 .. B loop
      if Smooth (i) mod P = 0 then
         Smooth (i) := Smooth (i) / P;
         if Smooth (i) mod P = 0 then
```

```
93              Sieve (i) := True;
94           end if;
95        end if;
96     end loop;
97  end loop;
98  for i in 1 .. B loop
99     if Smooth (i) /= 1 then
100        return Factor;
101     end if;
102  end loop;
103  for i in 1 .. B loop
104     for j in 1 .. B loop
105        if Is_Square (Smooth (i) * Smooth (j)) then
106           A := Sqrt (Smooth (i) * Smooth (j));
107           P := Gcd (A - Sqrt (Smooth (i)), N);
108           if P /= 1 and then P /= N then
109              Found : Boolean := False;
110              for k in 1 .. Factor'Length loop
111                 if Factor (k).Prime = P then
112                    Found := True;
113                    Factor (k).Power := Factor (k).Power + 1;
114                 end if;
115              end loop;
116              if not Found then
117                 Factor (Factor'Length + 1).Prime := P;
118                 Factor (Factor'Length + 1).Power := 1;
119              end if;
120              N := N / P;
121              if N = 1 then
122                 return Factor;
123              end if;
124           end if;
125        end if;
126     end loop;
127  end loop;
128 end Quadratic_Sieve;
```

The code uses the quadratic sieve algorithm to factorize a given integer N. It first calculates the square root of N and sets B to be the ceiling of the square root. It then calculates M as $B^2 - N$ and proceeds to find a sequence of M values until it finds a perfect square, i.e., until $Is\_Square(M)$ is true. The sequence of M values is stored in an array called Smooth.

The code then sieves the primes up to B using the Smooth array. For each prime P, it divides each Smooth value that is divisible by P by P until it is no longer divisible by P. If a Smooth value becomes divisible by P twice, it is marked as not being smooth, and the sieve continues with the next prime.

Once the sieving is complete, the code checks if all the Smooth values have been reduced to 1. If they haven't, it exits without finding any factors.

§ 3 Modular Arithemetic

There are no specific algorithms specifically beneficial enough when studied at the elementary level so we create our own basic algorithm for implementation:

```cpp
#include <iostream>
using namespace std;

// Function to perform modular addition
int mod_add(int a, int b, int m) {
    return (a % m + b % m) % m;
}

// Function to perform modular subtraction
int mod_sub(int a, int b, int m) {
    return ((a % m - b % m) % m + m) % m;
}

// Function to perform modular multiplication
int mod_mul(int a, int b, int m) {
    return ((a % m) * (b % m)) % m;
}

// Function to perform modular exponentiation
int mod_pow(int a, int b, int m) {
    int res = 1;
    while (b > 0) {
        if (b & 1) {
            res = mod_mul(res, a, m);
        }
        a = mod_mul(a, a, m);
        b >>= 1;
    }
    return res;
}

// Function to calculate modular inverse
int mod_inv(int a, int m) {
    int m0 = m, t, q;
    int x0 = 0, x1 = 1;

    if (m == 1) {
        return 0;
    }

    while (a > 1) {
        q = a / m;
        t = m;
        m = a % m, a = t;
        t = x0;
        x0 = x1 - q * x0;
        x1 = t;
```

```cpp
48      }
49
50      if (x1 < 0) {
51          x1 += m0;
52      }
53
54      return x1;
55  }
56
57  // Function to perform modular division
58  int mod_div(int a, int b, int m) {
59      a = a % m;
60      int inv = mod_inv(b, m);
61      if (inv == -1) {
62          cout << "Division not defined";
63          return -1;
64      }
65      else {
66          return mod_mul(a, inv, m);
67      }
68  }
69
70  int main() {
71      int a, b, m;
72      cout << "Enter values of a, b and m: ";
73      cin >> a >> b >> m;
74      cout << "Modular addition: " << mod_add(a, b, m) << endl;
75      cout << "Modular subtraction: " << mod_sub(a, b, m) << endl;
76      cout << "Modular multiplication: " << mod_mul(a, b, m) << endl;
77      cout << "Modular exponentiation: " << mod_pow(a, b, m) << endl;
78      cout << "Modular inverse: " << mod_inv(a, m) << endl;
79      cout << "Modular division: " << mod_div(a, b, m) << endl;
80      return 0;
81  }
```

§ 4   Diophantine Equations

We aim here to create an algorithm for equations in form of Ax + By = C. It can be implemented:

```ada
1  with Ada.Text_IO; use Ada.Text_IO;
2
3  procedure Diophantine is
4     X, Y, A, B, C: Integer;
5     Found: Boolean := False;
6  begin
7     Put("Enter values for A, B and C in the equation Ax + By = C: ");
8     Get(A); Get(B); Get(C);
9
10     for X in 1..C loop
```

```
11      Y := (C - A * X) / B;
12      if (C - A * X) mod B = 0 and Y > 0 then
13         Put("Solution: X = "); Put(X); Put(", Y = "); Put(Y);
14         Found := True;
15         exit;
16      end if;
17   end loop;
18
19   if not Found then
20      Put("No solutions exist for the given equation.");
21   end if;
22 end Diophantine;
```

This algorithm prompts the user to enter the values of A, B and C in the equation $Ax + By = C$. It then uses a loop to iterate through possible values of X, and calculates the corresponding value of Y using the equation $Y = (C - A * X)/B$. If the calculated value of Y is a positive integer, and the equation is satisfied for these values of X and Y, then the algorithm outputs the solution. If no solutions are found, the algorithm outputs a message indicating this.

You can extend this algorithm by adding more features, such as allowing the user to input negative values of X and Y, or by adding error checking for invalid input values.

§ 5   Continued Fraction

There are several ways to solve the algorithm for this. We can use Simple Continued Fraction Theorem as doing this implementation:

```
1  #include <stdio.h>
2
3  void simple_continued_fraction(double x, int n) {
4      int i;
5      double a;
6
7      printf("Simple continued fraction for %lf:\n[", x);
8
9      for (i = 0; i < n; i++) {
10         a = (int) x;      // integer part of x
11         x = 1 / (x - a);  // fractional part of x
12         printf("%d", (int) a);   // print integer part
13         if (i < n - 1) printf(", "); // print comma if not last term
14     }
15
16     printf("]\n");
17 }
18
19 int main() {
20     double x = 1.41421356;   // square root of 2
21     int n = 10;              // number of terms in continued fraction
22     simple_continued_fraction(x, n);
```

```ada
23        return 0;
24  }
```

In this implementation, the simple_continued_fraction function takes two arguments: the real number x for which we want to compute the continued fraction, and the number of terms n that we want to compute. The function uses a loop to compute each term in the continued fraction by computing the integer part a of x, subtracting a from x to get the fractional part, and then inverting the fractional part to get the next term. The loop then repeats this process for the desired number of terms. The resulting continued fraction is printed to the console in the form of a list enclosed in square brackets.

In the main function, we define the value of x to be the square root of 2, and the number of terms n to be 10. We then call the simple_continued_fraction function with these arguments to compute the continued fraction of the square root of 2.

Another interesting algorithm is Regular Continued Fraction Theorem, which can go on in ada as:

```ada
1  with Ada.Text_IO; use Ada.Text_IO;
2  with Ada.Integer_Text_IO; use Ada.Integer_Text_IO;
3
4  procedure Regular_Continued_Fraction is
5
6     function Continued_Fraction(X : Float; N : Integer) return Float is
7        A : Integer;
8        F : Float;
9     begin
10        if N = 0 then
11           return 0.0;
12        else
13           A := Integer(X);
14           F := X - Float(A);
15           return Float(A) + 1.0 / Continued_Fraction(F, N-1);
16        end if;
17     end Continued_Fraction;
18
19     X : Float := 3.14159265358979323846264338328;  -- pi
20     N : Integer := 10;  -- number of terms in continued fraction
21
22  begin
23     Put("Regular continued fraction for ");
24     Put(X, Exp => 0);
25     Put(": [");
26
27     for I in 1..N loop
28        Put(Integer(Continued_Fraction(X, I)));
29        if I < N then
30           Put(", ");
31        end if;
32     end loop;
33
34     Put_Line("]");
```

```
35 end Regular_Continued_Fraction;
```

In this implementation, the Continued_Fraction function takes two arguments: the real number X for which we want to compute the continued fraction, and the number of terms N that we want to compute. The function uses a recursive algorithm to compute each term in the continued fraction by computing the integer part A of X, subtracting A from X to get the fractional part F, and then recursively calling the function with F as the new X and N-1 as the new N. The function then returns the sum of A and the inverse of the result of the recursive call. The function returns 0.0 if N is 0.

In the Regular_Continued_Fraction procedure, we define the value of X to be pi, and the number of terms N to be 10. We then call the Continued_Fraction function in a loop to compute each term of the continued fraction, and print the result to the console in the form of a list enclosed in square brackets.

As a short code benefit, we can use the Euler Algorithm

```cpp
#include <iostream>
using namespace std;

int euclidean_algorithm(int a, int b) {
    int r;
    while (b != 0) {
        r = a % b;
        a = b;
        b = r;
    }
    return a;
}

int main() {
    int a = 1071, b = 462;
    int gcd = euclidean_algorithm(a, b);
    cout << "The GCD of " << a << " and " << b << " is " << gcd << endl;
    return 0;
}
```

In this implementation, the euclidean_algorithm function takes two arguments a and b as inputs and returns their greatest common divisor (GCD) using the Euclidean algorithm. The function uses a while loop to iterate through the algorithm, calculating the remainder r of a divided by b and then setting a to b and b to r. The loop continues until b is equal to 0, at which point the GCD of a and b is equal to a. The function then returns the GCD.

In the main function, we define the values of a and b to be 1071 and 462, respectively, and call the euclidean_algorithm function with these arguments to compute their GCD. We then print the result to the console using cout.

Another alternative that can be possibly used is Stern-Brocot Tree, which can be implemented as following:

```ada
with Ada.Text_IO; use Ada.Text_IO;
with Ada.Float_Text_IO; use Ada.Float_Text_IO;

```

```ada
procedure Stern_Brocot_Tree is

   type Fraction is record
      Numerator : Integer;
      Denominator : Integer;
   end record;

   function Add_Fractions(F1, F2 : Fraction) return Fraction is
      Result : Fraction;
   begin
      Result.Numerator := F1.Numerator * F2.Denominator + F2.Numerator *
   F1.Denominator;
      Result.Denominator := F1.Denominator * F2.Denominator;
      return Result;
   end Add_Fractions;

   function Simplify_Fraction(F : Fraction) return Fraction is
      GCD : Integer := Integer'Rem(F.Numerator, F.Denominator);
      Result : Fraction;
   begin
      while GCD /= 0 loop
         F.Numerator := F.Denominator;
         F.Denominator := GCD;
         GCD := Integer'Rem(F.Numerator, F.Denominator);
      end loop;
      Result.Numerator := F.Numerator / F.Denominator;
      Result.Denominator := 1;
      return Result;
   end Simplify_Fraction;

   procedure Print_Fraction(F : Fraction) is
   begin
      Put(F.Numerator, Width => 3);
      Put("/");
      Put(F.Denominator, Width => 3);
      Put(" ");
   end Print_Fraction;

   procedure Generate_Stern_Brocot_Tree(N : Integer) is
      Left, Right, Mid : Fraction;
   begin
      Left := (others => <>)(Numerator => 0, Denominator => 1);
      Right := (others => <>)(Numerator => 1, Denominator => 0);
      Print_Fraction(Left);
      for I in 1..N loop
         Mid := Simplify_Fraction(Add_Fractions(Left, Right));
         Print_Fraction(Mid);
         Left := Simplify_Fraction(Add_Fractions(Left, Mid));
         Right := Simplify_Fraction(Add_Fractions(Mid, Right));
      end loop;
      Print_Fraction(Right);
```

```
54    end Generate_Stern_Brocot_Tree;
55
56 begin
57    Generate_Stern_Brocot_Tree(10);
58    New_Line;
59 end Stern_Brocot_Tree;
```

In this implementation, we define a Fraction type that represents a fraction as a numerator and denominator. We also define two helper functions: Add_Fractions adds two fractions together, and Simplify_Fraction simplifies a fraction by dividing its numerator and denominator by their greatest common divisor. We also define a Print_Fraction procedure that prints a fraction to the console in the form of a fraction.

The main function of this program is Generate_Stern_Brocot_Tree, which takes an integer N as an argument and generates the first N levels of the Stern-Brocot tree. The function starts by initializing the left and right fractions to 0/1 and 1/0, respectively, and printing the left fraction to the console. It then enters a loop that generates each level of the tree by computing the middle fraction as the sum of the left and right fractions, simplifying the middle fraction, printing it to the console, and updating the left and right fractions to be the middle fraction and the original right fraction, respectively.

We can finally end up talking on the Wallis Algorithm to solve Continued Fraction Theorem with the following implementation in C:

```
1 #include <stdio.h>
2
3 int main() {
4     int i, n;
5     double pi = 1.0;
6     printf("Enter the number of terms in the Wallis formula: ");
7     scanf("%d", &n);
8     for (i = 1; i <= n; i++) {
9         pi *= (double) (4 * i * i) / (4 * i * i - 1);
10    }
11    pi *= 2;
12    printf("Pi estimated with %d terms of the Wallis formula: %f\n", n,
   pi);
13    return 0;
14 }
```

In this implementation, we first prompt the user to enter the number of terms they would like to use in the Wallis formula. We then initialize the variable pi to 1.0 and enter a loop that iterates n times, multiplying pi by the expression $(4i^2)/(4i^2 - 1)$ on each iteration. After the loop completes, we multiply pi by 2 to get the estimate of pi, and then print the estimate to the console.

Note that we cast the numerator and denominator of the expression $(4i^2)/(4i^2 - 1)$ to double in order to ensure that floating point division is performed instead of integer division, which would truncate the result.

§ 6   Quadratic Residue

We make an implementation of the quadratic residue algorithm in Ada. This code uses a long integer (Long_Integer) data type to handle large numbers.

```ada
with Ada.Text_IO; use Ada.Text_IO;

procedure Quadratic_Residue is

   -- Function to calculate the Legendre symbol
   function Legendre_Symbol (a, p : Long_Integer) return Long_Integer is
      begin
         if (a mod p) = 0 then
            return 0;
         elsif ((a**((p-1)/2)) mod p) = 1 then
            return 1;
         else
            return -1;
         end if;
      end Legendre_Symbol;

   -- Function to calculate the quadratic residue
   function Quadratic_Residue (n, p : Long_Integer) return Long_Integer
   is
      begin
         if Legendre_Symbol(n, p) /= 1 then
            return -1;
         else
            for i in 0 .. p-1 loop
               if ((i**2) mod p) = n then
                  return i;
               end if;
            end loop;
         end if;
         return -1;
      end Quadratic_Residue;

   -- Main program
   n : Long_Integer;
   p : Long_Integer := 101; -- The prime number
begin
   Put("Enter a number to find its quadratic residue: ");
   Get(n);

   -- Calculate the quadratic residue of n mod p
   Put("Quadratic residue of ");
   Put(n, 0);
   Put(" mod ");
   Put(p, 0);
   Put(" is ");
   Put(Quadratic_Residue(n mod p, p), 0);
   New_Line;
```

```
47  end Quadratic_Residue;
```

This code defines two functions: Legendre_Symbol and Quadratic_Residue. The Legendre_Symbol function calculates the Legendre symbol of a given number a and prime number p. The Quadratic_Residue function uses the Legendre symbol to determine whether n is a quadratic residue modulo p. If it is, the function returns the quadratic residue of n modulo p.

In the main program, the user is prompted to enter a number n to find its quadratic residue. The program then calculates the quadratic residue of n modulo a fixed prime number p (in this case, 101), using the Quadratic_Residue function.

Note that for large values of n and p, this algorithm can take a long time to compute, especially if the p value is very large. In practice, faster algorithms are used to compute quadratic residues for large values.

Chapter 2

Graph Theory

§ 1   Dijkstra's Algorithm

Here is an implementation of the algorithm in C++:

```cpp
#include <iostream>
#include <vector>
#include <queue>
#include <climits> // for INT_MAX

using namespace std;

typedef pair<int, int> iPair; // shorthand for (node, weight) pair

void dijkstra(vector<vector<iPair>>& graph, int start) {
    int num_nodes = graph.size();
    vector<int> dist(num_nodes, INT_MAX); // initialize all distances to infinity
    priority_queue<iPair, vector<iPair>, greater<iPair>> pq; // min heap priority queue to select next node

    dist[start] = 0; // distance to starting node is 0
    pq.push(make_pair(0, start)); // add starting node to priority queue

    while (!pq.empty()) {
        int u = pq.top().second; // select node with smallest distance
        pq.pop();

        // explore all adjacent nodes of u
        for (auto it = graph[u].begin(); it != graph[u].end(); it++) {
            int v = it->first;
            int weight = it->second;

            // if the distance to v through u is smaller than the current
distance to v, update it
            if (dist[u] + weight < dist[v]) {
                dist[v] = dist[u] + weight;
```

```cpp
                    pq.push(make_pair(dist[v], v)); // add v to priority
    queue to be explored later
            }
        }
    }

    // print the distances from start node to all other nodes
    cout << "Shortest distances from node " << start << ":\n";
    for (int i = 0; i < num_nodes; i++) {
        cout << i << ": " << dist[i] << endl;
    }
}

int main() {
    // create a graph with 5 nodes and 7 edges
    vector<vector<iPair>> graph(5);
    graph[0].push_back(make_pair(1, 2));
    graph[0].push_back(make_pair(3, 6));
    graph[1].push_back(make_pair(2, 3));
    graph[1].push_back(make_pair(3, 8));
    graph[1].push_back(make_pair(4, 5));
    graph[2].push_back(make_pair(4, 7));
    graph[3].push_back(make_pair(4, 9));

    dijkstra(graph, 0); // find shortest paths from node 0

    return 0;
}
```

In this implementation, graph is a vector of vectors representing the adjacency list of the graph. Each element of graph is a vector of pairs, where each pair represents an edge between two nodes and the weight of that edge. The function dijkstra takes graph and a starting node as input, and it outputs the shortest distances from the starting node to all other nodes.

The algorithm initializes all distances to infinity except for the starting node, whose distance is set to 0. It uses a priority queue to select the node with the smallest distance from the starting node, and it explores all adjacent nodes of that node to update their distances if a shorter path is found. This process continues until all reachable nodes have been explored.

Finally, the function prints the shortest distances from the starting node to all other nodes.

§ 2   Bellman-Ford Algorithm

We implement this in algorithmic form, continuing with ada as:

```ada
procedure Bellman_Ford (G : in Graph; start : in Node) is
    dist : array(Node) of Integer;
```

```
3      pred : array(Node) of Node;
4  begin
5      -- Step 1: Initialize distances and predecessors
6      for v in G.nodes loop
7          dist(v) := MAX_INT;
8          pred(v) := null;
9      end loop;
10     dist(start) := 0;
11
12     -- Step 2: Relax all edges |V| - 1 times
13     for i in 1 .. G.nodes'Length - 1 loop
14         for e in G.edges loop
15             u := e.source;
16             v := e.destination;
17             weight := e.weight;
18             if dist(u) + weight < dist(v) then
19                 dist(v) := dist(u) + weight;
20                 pred(v) := u;
21             end if;
22         end loop;
23     end loop;
24
25     -- Step 3: Check for negative-weight cycles
26     for e in G.edges loop
27         u := e.source;
28         v := e.destination;
29         weight := e.weight;
30         if dist(u) + weight < dist(v) then
31             raise Negative_Weight_Cycle_Exception;
32         end if;
33     end loop;
34
35     -- Print the shortest path distances and predecessors from start node
         to all other nodes
36     Put_Line("Shortest path distances from node " & start & ":");
37     for v in G.nodes loop
38         Put(v & ": " & dist(v));
39     end loop;
40
41     Put_Line("Predecessors from node " & start & ":");
42     for v in G.nodes loop
43         Put(v & ": " & pred(v));
44     end loop;
45  end Bellman_Ford;
```

In this implementation, G is a user-defined record type representing a graph, where G.nodes is an array of nodes and G.edges is an array of edges. Each edge is a record type containing a source node, a destination node, and a weight. The function Bellman_Ford takes G and a starting node as input, and it outputs the shortest path distances and predecessors from the starting node to all other nodes.

The algorithm first initializes all distances to infinity except for the starting node, whose distance is set to 0. It also initializes all predecessors to null. It then relaxes all edges $\|V\| - 1$ times, where $\|V\|$ is the number of nodes in the graph. This is to ensure that all shortest paths have been found, since the shortest path between any two nodes contains at most $\|V\| - 1$ edges.

After relaxing all edges, the algorithm checks for negative-weight cycles. If there is a negative-weight cycle, the algorithm raises an exception, since it is not possible to find a shortest path in a graph with a negative-weight cycle.

Finally, the function prints the shortest path distances and predecessors from the starting node to all other nodes.

§ 3   Floyd-Warshall Algorithm

We implement this algorithm in Fortran:

```fortran
program Floyd_Warshall(G, num_nodes)
    implicit none

    integer, parameter :: MAX_INT = 1000000
    integer, intent(in) :: num_nodes
    integer, dimension(num_nodes, num_nodes), intent(inout) :: G

    integer :: i, j, k

    ! Step 1: Initialize the distance matrix
    do i = 1, num_nodes
        do j = 1, num_nodes
            if (i == j) then
                G(i,j) = 0
            else if (G(i,j) == 0) then
                G(i,j) = MAX_INT
            end if
        end do
    end do

    ! Step 2: Compute shortest paths using dynamic programming
    do k = 1, num_nodes
        do i = 1, num_nodes
            do j = 1, num_nodes
                if (G(i,k) + G(k,j) < G(i,j)) then
                    G(i,j) = G(i,k) + G(k,j)
                end if
            end do
        end do
    end do

    ! Step 3: Output the shortest path distances
    write(*,*) "Shortest path distances between nodes:"
    do i = 1, num_nodes
        do j = 1, num_nodes
```

```
36        if (G(i,j) == MAX_INT) then
37            write(*,"(A,I3,A,I3,A)") "Node ", i, " and node ", j, "
     are not connected"
38            else
39            write(*,"(A,I3,A,I3,A,I6)") "Distance between node ", i,
     " and node ", j, " is ", G(i,j)
40        end if
41     end do
42   end do
43 end program Floyd_Warshall
```

In this implementation, G is a two-dimensional array representing the adjacency matrix of the graph, and num_nodes is the number of nodes in the graph. The algorithm outputs the shortest path distances between all pairs of nodes.

The algorithm first initializes the distance matrix G by setting the distance between each node and itself to 0, and setting the distance between any two nodes that are not connected to a large value (in this case, MAX_INT).

It then uses dynamic programming to compute the shortest path distances between all pairs of nodes. The algorithm iterates through each intermediate node k and updates the distance matrix G by considering whether the path from i to j through k is shorter than the current path from i to j.

Finally, the algorithm outputs the shortest path distances between all pairs of nodes. If two nodes are not connected, the output indicates that they are not connected. Otherwise, the output indicates the distance between the two nodes.

§ 4   Kruskal's Algorithm

We can implement it in GDW-Basic as follows:

```
10 ' Implementation of Kruskal's algorithm in GDW-Basic
20 ' Input: An undirected, weighted graph G with n nodes and m edges
30 ' Output: A minimum spanning tree of G

40 ' Initialize the graph
50 DIM G(100,100)
60 INPUT "Enter the number of nodes: ", n
70 FOR i = 1 TO n
80   FOR j = 1 TO n
90     G(i,j) = 0
100    NEXT j
110 NEXT i

120 ' Input the edges and their weights
130 INPUT "Enter the number of edges: ", m
140 FOR i = 1 TO m
150   INPUT "Enter edge (u,v) and weight: ", u, v, w
160   G(u,v) = w
170   G(v,u) = w ' Assume graph is undirected
```

```
180 NEXT i

190 ' Initialize the disjoint sets
200 DIM parent(100)
210 FOR i = 1 TO n
220   parent(i) = i
230 NEXT i

240 ' Sort the edges by weight
250 DIM edges(10000, 2)
260 k = 1
270 FOR i = 1 TO n
280   FOR j = i+1 TO n
290     IF G(i,j) > 0 THEN
300       edges(k,1) = i
310       edges(k,2) = j
320       edges(k,3) = G(i,j)
330       k = k + 1
340     END IF
350   NEXT j
360 NEXT i
370 CALL QuickSort(edges, 1, k-1, 3)

380 ' Run Kruskal's algorithm
390 DIM MST(100,100)
400 num_edges = 0
410 FOR i = 1 TO k-1
420   u = edges(i,1)
430   v = edges(i,2)
440   w = edges(i,3)
450   ' Check if adding this edge creates a cycle
460   IF Find(u) <> Find(v) THEN
470     Union(u, v)
480     num_edges = num_edges + 1
490     MST(u,v) = w
500     MST(v,u) = w ' Assume graph is undirected
510     ' Stop when the MST has n-1 edges
520     IF num_edges = n-1 THEN EXIT FOR
530   END IF
540 NEXT i

550 ' Output the MST
560 PRINT "Minimum Spanning Tree:"
570 FOR i = 1 TO n
580   FOR j = i+1 TO n
590     IF MST(i,j) > 0 THEN
600       PRINT i; "-" ; j; ": " ; MST(i,j)
610     END IF
620   NEXT j
630 NEXT i
```

```
640 ' Subroutines for disjoint set operations
650 FUNCTION Find(x)
660    IF parent(x) = x THEN
670       RETURN x
680    ELSE
690       RETURN Find(parent(x))
700    END IF
710 END FUNCTION

720 SUB Union(x, y)
730    parent(Find(x)) = Find(y)
740 END SUB
```

In this implementation, the input graph G is represented as a two-dimensional array, and the output minimum spanning tree MST is also represented as a two-dimensional array. The algorithm uses a quicksort implementation to sort the edges of the graph by weight and then iterates through them, adding edges to the MST if they do not create a cycle.

§ 5   Prim's Algorithm

We begin with the algorithm implementation in Java as follows:

```java
import java.util.*;

public class Prim {
    public static void main(String[] args) {
        Scanner input = new Scanner(System.in);
        int n, m; // n: number of nodes, m: number of edges
        int[][] graph; // graph represented as adjacency matrix

        // Read input graph
        System.out.print("Enter number of nodes: ");
        n = input.nextInt();
        graph = new int[n][n];
        System.out.print("Enter number of edges: ");
        m = input.nextInt();
        for (int i = 0; i < m; i++) {
            int u, v, w;
            System.out.print("Enter edge (u v w): ");
            u = input.nextInt();
            v = input.nextInt();
            w = input.nextInt();
            graph[u][v] = w;
            graph[v][u] = w; // assume graph is undirected
        }

        // Initialize minimum spanning tree
        int[] parent = new int[n]; // parent[i] stores the parent of node
    i in the MST
```

```
27        int[] key = new int[n]; // key[i] stores the minimum weight edge
     connecting node i to the MST
28        boolean[] visited = new boolean[n]; // visited[i] is true if node
      i has been added to the MST
29        Arrays.fill(key, Integer.MAX_VALUE); // initialize all keys to
     infinity
30        key[0] = 0; // start with node 0
31
32        // Run Prim's algorithm
33        for (int i = 0; i < n-1; i++) { // MST has n-1 edges
34            // Find the node with the minimum key that has not been added
     to the MST
35            int u = -1;
36            for (int j = 0; j < n; j++) {
37                if (!visited[j] && (u == -1 || key[j] < key[u])) {
38                    u = j;
39                }
40            }
41
42            visited[u] = true;
43
44            // Update the keys and parents of neighboring nodes
45            for (int v = 0; v < n; v++) {
46                if (graph[u][v] > 0 && !visited[v] && graph[u][v] < key[v
     ]) {
47                    parent[v] = u;
48                    key[v] = graph[u][v];
49                }
50            }
51        }
52
53        // Output the MST
54        System.out.println("Minimum Spanning Tree:");
55        for (int i = 1; i < n; i++) {
56            System.out.println(parent[i] + " - " + i + " : " + graph[
     parent[i]][i]);
57        }
58    }
59 }
```

In this implementation, the input graph graph is represented as a two-dimensional array, and the output minimum spanning tree is represented by the parent array, where parent[i] stores the parent of node i in the MST. The algorithm uses a visited array to keep track of which nodes have been added to the MST and a key array to store the minimum weight edge connecting each node to the MST.

The algorithm first reads in the input graph from the user and initializes the minimum spanning tree data structures. It then iterates through n-1 nodes, adding one node to the MST in each iteration. In each iteration, it finds the node with the minimum key that has not been added to the MST and adds it to the MST. It then updates the keys and parents of its neighboring nodes.

§ 6 Topological Sorting

An implementation of this algorithm is written in Julia as:

```julia
# Function to perform topological sorting
function topological_sort(graph)
    n = size(graph, 1) # number of nodes in the graph
    visited = zeros(Bool, n) # array to keep track of visited nodes
    stack = Vector{Int}() # stack to store nodes in topological order

    # Recursive function to visit nodes
    function visit(node)
        visited[node] = true

        # Recursively visit all neighbors
        for neighbor in findall(graph[node, :])
            if !visited[neighbor]
                visit(neighbor)
            end
        end

        # Add node to stack after all its neighbors have been visited
        push!(stack, node)
    end

    # Visit all unvisited nodes in the graph
    for node in 1:n
        if !visited[node]
            visit(node)
        end
    end

    return reverse(stack) # return the stack in reverse order to get
    topological order
end

# Example usage
graph = [0 0 0 0 0 0;
         1 0 0 0 0 0;
         1 1 0 0 0 0;
         0 1 1 0 0 0;
         0 0 1 1 0 0;
         0 0 0 1 1 0]

order = topological_sort(graph)
println("Topological order: ", order)
```

In this implementation, the input graph "graph" is represented as a two-dimensional array, where graph[i, j] = 1 if there is a directed edge from node i to node j. The output of the function is an array order containing the nodes in topological order.

The algorithm works by visiting each node in the graph and recursively visiting all its neighbors. It keeps track of which nodes have been visited using the visited array and adds nodes to the stack after all their neighbors have been visited. The resulting stack contains the nodes in reverse topological order, so the function returns the reversed stack to obtain the topological order.

In the example usage, the function is called with an example graph represented as an adjacency matrix. The output of the function is the topological order of the nodes, which is [6, 5, 4, 3, 2, 1]. This corresponds to the ordering 6 -¿ 5 -¿ 4 -¿ 3 -¿ 2 -¿ 1 of the nodes in the directed acyclic graph represented by the adjacency matrix.

§ 7   Depth-First Search

Here's an implementation of Depth-First Search (DFS) in C++:

```cpp
#include <iostream>
#include <vector>
#include <stack>

using namespace std;

// Function to perform DFS
void dfs(vector<vector<int>>& graph, vector<bool>& visited, int node) {
    visited[node] = true; // Mark current node as visited
    cout << node << " "; // Print current node

    // Recursively visit all unvisited neighbors
    for (int neighbor : graph[node]) {
        if (!visited[neighbor]) {
            dfs(graph, visited, neighbor);
        }
    }
}

int main() {
    int n = 7; // Number of nodes in the graph
    vector<vector<int>> graph(n); // Adjacency list to represent graph
    graph[0] = {1, 2};
    graph[1] = {0, 2, 3, 4};
    graph[2] = {0, 1, 5};
    graph[3] = {1, 4};
    graph[4] = {1, 3};
    graph[5] = {2, 6};
    graph[6] = {5};

    vector<bool> visited(n, false); // Array to keep track of visited
    nodes
    int start = 0; // Starting node for DFS

    // Perform DFS from the starting node
    cout << "DFS traversal: ";
```

```
36      dfs(graph, visited, start);
37
38      return 0;
39  }
```

In this implementation, the input graph graph is represented as an adjacency list, where graph[i] is a vector containing the neighbors of node i. The output of the function is a DFS traversal of the graph, starting from the specified starting node.

The algorithm works by recursively visiting all unvisited neighbors of the current node, marking each visited node as it is visited, and printing each visited node. It keeps track of which nodes have been visited using the visited array.

In the example usage, the function is called with an example graph represented as an adjacency list. The output of the function is a DFS traversal of the graph starting from node 0, which is 0 1 2 5 6 3 4. This corresponds to the ordering in which the nodes are visited in the depth-first search of the graph represented by the adjacency list.

§ 8   Breadth-first Search

Here is an implementation we can do in C++:

```cpp
1  #include <iostream>
2  #include <vector>
3  #include <queue>
4
5  using namespace std;
6
7  // Function to perform BFS
8  void bfs(vector<vector<int>>& graph, vector<bool>& visited, int start) {
9      queue<int> q; // Queue to keep track of nodes to visit
10     q.push(start); // Add starting node to the queue
11     visited[start] = true; // Mark starting node as visited
12
13     while (!q.empty()) {
14         int node = q.front(); // Get the next node to visit
15         q.pop(); // Remove node from queue
16         cout << node << " "; // Print current node
17
18         // Visit all unvisited neighbors of the current node
19         for (int neighbor : graph[node]) {
20             if (!visited[neighbor]) {
21                 visited[neighbor] = true; // Mark neighbor as visited
22                 q.push(neighbor); // Add neighbor to queue
23             }
24         }
25     }
26 }
27
28 int main() {
29     int n = 7; // Number of nodes in the graph
```

```cpp
vector<vector<int>> graph(n); // Adjacency list to represent graph
graph[0] = {1, 2};
graph[1] = {0, 2, 3, 4};
graph[2] = {0, 1, 5};
graph[3] = {1, 4};
graph[4] = {1, 3};
graph[5] = {2, 6};
graph[6] = {5};

vector<bool> visited(n, false); // Array to keep track of visited
    nodes
int start = 0; // Starting node for BFS

// Perform BFS from the starting node
cout << "BFS traversal: ";
bfs(graph, visited, start);

return 0;
}
```

In this implementation, the input graph graph is represented as an adjacency list, where graph[i] is a vector containing the neighbors of node i. The output of the function is a BFS traversal of the graph, starting from the specified starting node.

The algorithm works by maintaining a queue of nodes to visit, initially containing only the starting node. It repeatedly takes the next node from the front of the queue, visits all unvisited neighbors of the current node, adds them to the back of the queue, and marks them as visited. It continues until the queue is empty.

In the example usage, the function is called with an example graph represented as an adjacency list. The output of the function is a BFS traversal of the graph starting from node 0, which is 0 1 2 3 4 5 6. This corresponds to the ordering in which the nodes are visited in the breadth-first search of the graph represented by the adjacency list.

§ 9　Tarjan's Algorithm

We do an implementation for this in Fortran as:

```fortran
program tarjan_scc

implicit none

integer, parameter :: max_nodes = 1000 ! Maximum number of nodes in the
    graph

integer :: n ! Number of nodes in the graph
integer :: m ! Number of edges in the graph
integer :: i, u, v, index
integer :: time ! Counter for DFS discovery times
integer :: scc_count ! Counter for SCCs
integer :: node_stack(max_nodes) ! Stack to keep track of nodes
```

```fortran
13  integer :: low(max_nodes) ! Lowlink values of nodes
14  integer :: disc(max_nodes) ! Discovery times of nodes
15  integer :: on_stack(max_nodes) ! Flag for whether a node is on the stack
16  integer :: head(max_nodes) ! Head of the adjacency list for each node
17  integer :: next(max_nodes) ! Next index in the adjacency list
18  integer :: to(max_nodes) ! Destination node of each edge in the adjacency
        list
19
20  integer, allocatable :: stack_scc(:) ! SCCs found during the algorithm
21  integer, allocatable :: scc_size(:) ! Sizes of the SCCs found
22
23  ! Read input graph
24  read(*,*) n, m
25  allocate(head(0:n), next(0:m), to(0:m))
26  do i = 0, n-1
27      head(i) = -1
28  end do
29  do i = 1, m
30      read(*,*) u, v
31      next(i) = head(u)
32      to(i) = v
33      head(u) = i
34  end do
35
36  ! Initialize algorithm variables
37  time = 0
38  scc_count = 0
39  index = 0
40  allocate(on_stack(0:n), disc(0:n), low(0:n), node_stack(0:n))
41  on_stack = 0
42  disc = -1
43
44  ! Perform Tarjan's algorithm
45  do i = 0, n-1
46      if (disc(i) == -1) then
47          call tarjan_scc_recursive(i, head, next, to, disc, low,
        node_stack, on_stack, index, time, scc_count, stack_scc)
48      end if
49  end do
50
51  ! Count sizes of the SCCs
52  allocate(scc_size(0:scc_count-1))
53  scc_size = 0
54  do i = 0, size(stack_scc)-1
55      scc_size(stack_scc(i)) = scc_size(stack_scc(i)) + 1
56  end do
57
58  ! Print the SCCs and their sizes
59  do i = 0, scc_count-1
60      write(*,*) "SCC ", i, ": size = ", scc_size(i)
61      do u = 0, n-1
```

```fortran
            if (stack_scc(u) == i) then
                write(*,*) " ", u
            end if
        end do
end do

contains

! Recursive subroutine for Tarjan's algorithm
subroutine tarjan_scc_recursive(u, head, next, to, disc, low, node_stack, &
        on_stack, index, time, scc_count, stack_scc)
    integer, intent(in) :: u, head(:), next(:), to(:), time
    integer, intent(inout) :: disc(:), low(:), node_stack(:), on_stack(:) &
        , index, scc_count
    integer, allocatable, intent(inout) :: stack_scc(:)
    integer :: v, e

    disc(u) = time
    low(u) = time
    time = time + 1
node_stack(index) = u
on_stack(u) = 1

! Traverse the adjacency list of the node
e = head(u)
do while (e /= -1)
    v = to(e)
    if (disc(v) == -1) then
        ! Recurse on the unvisited neighbor
        call tarjan_scc_recursive(v, head, next, to, disc, low, &
    node_stack, on_stack, index, time, scc_count, stack_scc)
        low(u) = min(low(u), low(v))
    else if (on_stack(v) == 1) then
        ! Update the lowlink value of the node
        low(u) = min(low(u), disc(v))
    end if
    e = next(e)
end do

! If the node is the root of an SCC, pop the SCC off the stack
if (low(u) == disc(u)) then
    do while (node_stack(index) /= u)
        stack_scc(node_stack(index)) = scc_count
        on_stack(node_stack(index)) = 0
        index = index - 1
    end do
    stack_scc(u) = scc_count
    on_stack(u) = 0
    index = index - 1
    scc_count = scc_count + 1
end if
```

```
110 end subroutine tarjan_scc_recursive
111
112 end program tarjan_scc
```

In this implementation, we first read in the input graph from standard input. We then initialize the algorithm variables and perform Tarjan's algorithm on each unvisited node in the graph. The main algorithm is implemented as a recursive subroutine 'tarjan_scc_recursive', which takes as input a node 'u' and updates the discovery time and lowlink value of 'u', and recursively calls itself on each unvisited neighbor of 'u'. The algorithm uses a stack 'node_stack' to keep track of the nodes visited in the current SCC, and a flag 'on_stack' to indicate whether a node is currently on the stack. When a node is determined to be the root of an SCC, the algorithm pops the SCC off the stack and assigns it a new index in the 'stack_scc' array.

After the algorithm has finished, we count the sizes of the SCCs by iterating over the 'stack_scc' array, and print out each SCC and its size. Note that in Fortran, array indices start at 1, so we use '0:n' and '0:m' in the array declarations to make sure we have enough space to store all the nodes and edges.

§ 10   Minimum Cut

Here is an implementation of the Karger's algorithm for finding minimum cut in a graph, in C++:

```cpp
1 #include <bits/stdc++.h>
2 using namespace std;
3
4 // Returns a random integer between min and max (inclusive)
5 int random(int min, int max) {
6     return min + rand() % (max - min + 1);
7 }
8
9 // Finds the minimum cut of a graph using Karger's algorithm
10 int min_cut(vector<vector<int>>& graph) {
11     int n = graph.size();
12
13     // Contract edges until only 2 vertices remain
14     while (n > 2) {
15         // Choose a random edge
16         int u = random(0, n - 1);
17         int v = random(0, graph[u].size() - 1);
18         int w = graph[u][v];
19
20         // Merge u and w
21         for (int i = 0; i < graph[w].size(); i++) {
22             int x = graph[w][i];
23             if (x != u) {
24                 graph[u].push_back(x);
25                 graph[x].push_back(u);
```

```
26              }
27          }
28
29          // Remove w and its edges
30          graph[w].clear();
31          for (int i = 0; i < graph.size(); i++) {
32              for (int j = 0; j < graph[i].size(); j++) {
33                  if (graph[i][j] == w) {
34                      graph[i].erase(graph[i].begin() + j);
35                      break;
36                  }
37              }
38          }
39
40          n--;
41      }
42
43      // Return the size of the cut
44      return graph[0].size();
45  }
46
47  int main() {
48      int n, m;
49      cin >> n >> m;
50
51      // Read in the graph
52      vector<vector<int>> graph(n);
53      for (int i = 0; i < m; i++) {
54          int u, v;
55          cin >> u >> v;
56          graph[u].push_back(v);
57          graph[v].push_back(u);
58      }
59
60      // Run Karger's algorithm multiple times to increase the probability
    of finding the minimum cut
61      int num_runs = n * n * log(n);
62      int min_cut_size = n;
63      for (int i = 0; i < num_runs; i++) {
64          min_cut_size = min(min_cut_size, min_cut(graph));
65      }
66
67      cout << "Minimum cut size: " << min_cut_size << endl;
68
69      return 0;
70  }
```

In this implementation, we first read in the input graph from standard input and store it as an adjacency list graph. We then repeatedly run Karger's algorithm to find the minimum cut, and return the smallest cut size found over all runs. The min_cut function takes as input a graph represented as an adjacency list, and repeatedly chooses a random edge to contract until only 2 vertices remain. The function returns the size of the cut (i.e., the number of edges between the two remaining vertices).

To choose a random edge, we use the random function which returns a random integer between a given range. We then merge the vertices u and w by adding all the neighbors of w to u, and removing w and its edges from the graph. We repeat this process until only 2 vertices remain, and return the size of the cut.

Finally, in the main function, we run Karger's algorithm multiple times to increase the probability of finding the minimum cut. The number of runs is set to $n^2 * log(n)$, where n is the number of vertices in the graph. After running the algorithm, we print out the size of the minimum cut found.

Chapter 3

Probability Theory

§ 1   Monte Carlo Simulation

Here's an implementation of Monte Carlo simulation in Julia with an explanation:

```julia
function monte_carlo_simulation(n::Int, f::Function, bounds::Array{T,2})
    where T <: Real
    # n is the number of samples
    # f is the function to integrate
    # bounds is a 2D array specifying the bounds for each dimension of
    the integral

    # Initialize variables
    volume = prod(bounds[:,2] - bounds[:,1])  # total volume of the
    integration region
    sum_f = 0.0  # sum of function values inside the integration region
    sum_f_squared = 0.0  # sum of function values squared inside the
    integration region

    # Generate n random samples within the integration region
    for i in 1:n
        x = [rand()*(bounds[j,2]-bounds[j,1])+bounds[j,1] for j in 1:size
    (bounds,1)]
        # Evaluate the function at the random sample and update the sums
        fx = f(x)
        sum_f += fx
        sum_f_squared += fx^2
    end

    # Calculate the mean and variance of the function values
    mean_f = sum_f/n
    var_f = sum_f_squared/n - mean_f^2

    # Calculate the integral estimate and its error
    integral = mean_f * volume
    error = sqrt(var_f/n) * volume

```

```
28    return (integral, error)
29 end
```

The monte_carlo_simulation function takes three arguments: n, f, and bounds.

n specifies the number of random samples to generate. The more samples, the more accurate the integral estimate will be.

f is the function to integrate. It should take a single argument, which is an array of n random samples generated within the integration region.

bounds is a 2D array that specifies the lower and upper bounds for each dimension of the integration region. For example, if the integration region is a square with sides of length 2 centered at the origin, bounds could be [-1 1; -1 1].

The function first calculates the total volume of the integration region by taking the product of the lengths of each dimension. It then initializes variables to keep track of the sum of function values and the sum of function values squared within the integration region.

It then generates n random samples within the integration region by using the rand() function to generate a random number between 0 and 1, scaling it to the appropriate range for each dimension, and adding the lower bound for that dimension.

For each random sample, the function evaluates f at that point and updates the sum of function values and sum of function values squared variables.

After all samples have been generated, the function calculates the mean and variance of the function values. The mean is simply the sum of function values divided by n. The variance is calculated by subtracting the square of the mean from the sum of function values squared divided by n.

Finally, the function calculates the integral estimate by multiplying the mean function value by the volume of the integration region. It also calculates the error of the estimate by multiplying the standard deviation of the function values (which is the square root of the variance) by the volume of the integration region, divided by the square root of n.

To use the function, simply call it with the desired number of samples, function to integrate, and integration region bounds. For example:

```
1 f(x) = x[1]^2 + x[2]^2  # function to integrate (example: circle of
    radius 1 centered at
```

§ 2   Bayes' Theorem

We can implement it in C++:

```cpp
1 #include <iostream>
2 #include <vector>
3
4 using namespace std;
5
6 double bayes_theorem(double prior, double likelihood, double evidence) {
7     // Calculate posterior probability using Bayes' Theorem
```

```
 8      double posterior = (likelihood * prior) / evidence;
 9      return posterior;
10  }
11
12  int main() {
13      // Define prior probability, likelihood, and evidence
14      double prior = 0.1;
15      double likelihood = 0.8;
16      double evidence = 0.14;
17
18      // Calculate posterior probability using Bayes' Theorem
19      double posterior = bayes_theorem(prior, likelihood, evidence);
20
21      // Output posterior probability
22      cout << "Posterior probability: " << posterior << endl;
23
24      return 0;
25  }
```

The bayes_theorem function takes three arguments: prior, likelihood, and evidence.

prior is the prior probability of the hypothesis being true. It represents our belief about the hypothesis before we consider any new evidence.

likelihood is the likelihood of the evidence given the hypothesis. It represents how likely the evidence is to occur if the hypothesis is true.

evidence is the marginal likelihood of the evidence. It represents the total probability of the evidence occurring, regardless of whether the hypothesis is true or not.

The function calculates the posterior probability using Bayes' Theorem, which states that:

```
P(hypothesis | evidence) = P(evidence | hypothesis) * P(hypothesis) / P(
    evidence)
```

where P(hypothesis — evidence) is the posterior probability of the hypothesis given the evidence, P(evidence — hypothesis) is the likelihood of the evidence given the hypothesis, P(hypothesis) is the prior probability of the hypothesis, and P(evidence) is the marginal likelihood of the evidence.

In the bayes_theorem function, the posterior probability is calculated using this formula and returned.

In the main function, the prior probability, likelihood, and evidence are defined. These values are arbitrary and can be changed to reflect different scenarios.

The bayes_theorem function is then called with these values to calculate the posterior probability.

Finally, the posterior probability is output to the console using cout.

§ 3   Markov Chain Monte Carlo

Here's an example implementation of the Metropolis-Hastings Markov Chain Monte Carlo
algorithm in Fortran:

```fortran
program mcmc

    implicit none

    integer, parameter :: n = 10000 ! number of iterations
    real, parameter :: delta = 0.1 ! proposal standard deviation
    real, parameter :: pi = 3.14159265358979323846264338328 ! value of pi

    real :: x, y, x_proposal, y_proposal, acceptance_ratio, u
    integer :: i

    ! initial values
    x = 0.0
    y = 0.0

    ! loop over iterations
    do i = 1, n

        ! generate proposal
        call random_number(u)
        x_proposal = x + delta * (2.0 * u - 1.0)
        call random_number(u)
        y_proposal = y + delta * (2.0 * u - 1.0)

        ! calculate acceptance ratio
        acceptance_ratio = exp(-0.5 * ((x_proposal**2 + y_proposal**2) - &
    (x**2 + y**2))) / &
            exp(-0.5 * ((x**2 + y**2) - (x_proposal**2 + y_proposal**2)))

        ! generate acceptance probability
        call random_number(u)

        ! accept or reject proposal
        if (u <= acceptance_ratio) then
            x = x_proposal
            y = y_proposal
        end if

        ! output current state
        write(*,*) x, y

    end do

end program mcmc
```

This implementation uses the Metropolis-Hastings algorithm to sample from a Gaussian
distribution centered at the origin with standard deviation 1. The algorithm generates a

sequence of samples, where each sample is obtained by proposing a new state based on the current state and accepting or rejecting the proposed state based on an acceptance probability.

The program begins by setting the number of iterations (n) and the proposal standard deviation (delta). It also defines the value of pi (pi) for use later in the program.

The initial state is set to (0.0, 0.0).

The program then enters a loop over n iterations. For each iteration, a new state is proposed by generating a random number between 0 and 1 (u) and using it to modify the current state. The modified state is then compared to the current state using an acceptance ratio that depends on the Gaussian distribution. The acceptance ratio is calculated using the formula exp(-0.5 * ((x_proposal**2 + y_proposal**2) - (x**2 + y**2))) / exp(-0.5 * ((x**2 + y**2) - (x_proposal**2 + y_proposal**2))). If the acceptance ratio is greater than or equal to u, the proposed state is accepted; otherwise, it is rejected and the current state is retained.

At each iteration, the current state is output to the console using the write(*,*) statement.

This program can be modified to sample from other distributions by changing the acceptance ratio and proposal distribution.

§ 4   Gaussian Mixture Model

Here's an example implementation of the Gaussian Mixture Model in Java:

```java
import java.util.Arrays;
import java.util.Random;

public class GaussianMixtureModel {

    private final int k; // number of clusters
    private final int n; // number of data points
    private final double[] mu; // cluster means
    private final double[] sigma; // cluster standard deviations
    private final double[] pi; // cluster weights

    public GaussianMixtureModel(int k, int n) {
        this.k = k;
        this.n = n;
        this.mu = new double[k];
        this.sigma = new double[k];
        this.pi = new double[k];
    }

    public void fit(double[] data) {
        // initialize cluster parameters
        Random rand = new Random();
        for (int i = 0; i < k; i++) {
            mu[i] = data[rand.nextInt(n)];
```

```
25                sigma[i] = 1.0;
26                pi[i] = 1.0 / k;
27            }
28
29        // run EM algorithm
30        double[] w = new double[k];
31        double[] z = new double[n * k];
32        double[] new_mu = new double[k];
33        double[] new_sigma = new double[k];
34        double[] new_pi = new double[k];
35        double eps = 1e-6;
36        double log_likelihood = Double.NEGATIVE_INFINITY;
37        double new_log_likelihood = 0.0;
38        while (new_log_likelihood - log_likelihood > eps) {
39            log_likelihood = new_log_likelihood;
40
41            // E-step: calculate responsibilities
42            for (int i = 0; i < n; i++) {
43                double sum_w = 0.0;
44                for (int j = 0; j < k; j++) {
45                    w[j] = pi[j] * gaussian(data[i], mu[j], sigma[j]);
46                    sum_w += w[j];
47                }
48                for (int j = 0; j < k; j++) {
49                    z[i * k + j] = w[j] / sum_w;
50                }
51            }
52
53            // M-step: update parameters
54            for (int j = 0; j < k; j++) {
55                double sum_z = 0.0;
56                double sum_zx = 0.0;
57                for (int i = 0; i < n; i++) {
58                    sum_z += z[i * k + j];
59                    sum_zx += z[i * k + j] * data[i];
60                }
61                new_mu[j] = sum_zx / sum_z;
62                double sum_zxx = 0.0;
63                for (int i = 0; i < n; i++) {
64                    sum_zxx += z[i * k + j] * (data[i] - new_mu[j]) * (
    data[i] - new_mu[j]);
65                }
66                new_sigma[j] = Math.sqrt(sum_zxx / sum_z);
67                new_pi[j] = sum_z / n;
68            }
69
70            // calculate log-likelihood
71            new_log_likelihood = 0.0;
72            for (int i = 0; i < n; i++) {
73                double sum = 0.0;
74                for (int j = 0; j < k; j++) {
```

```
75                          sum += pi[j] * gaussian(data[i], mu[j], sigma[j]);
76                      }
77                      new_log_likelihood += Math.log(sum);
78                  }
79              }
80
81              // set new parameters
82              System.arraycopy(new_mu, 0, mu, 0, k);
83              System.arraycopy(new_sigma, 0, sigma, 0, k);
84              System.arraycopy(new_pi, 0, pi, 0, k);
85      }
86      private double gaussian(double x, double mu, double sigma) {
87          double norm = 1.0 / Math.sqrt(2 * Math.PI * sigma * sigma);
88          double exponent = -1.0 * (x - mu) * (x - mu) / (2 * sigma * sigma);
89          return norm * Math.exp(exponent);
90      }
91
92      public int predict(double x) {
93          double max_prob = Double.NEGATIVE_INFINITY;
94          int max_idx = -1;
95          for (int i = 0; i < k; i++) {
96              double prob = pi[i] * gaussian(x, mu[i], sigma[i]);
97              if (prob > max_prob) {
98                  max_prob = prob;
99                  max_idx = i;
100             }
101         }
102         return max_idx;
103     }
104
105     public static void main(String[] args) {
106         // generate data
107         Random rand = new Random();
108         int n = 1000;
109         double[] data = new double[n];
110         for (int i = 0; i < n; i++) {
111             if (rand.nextDouble() < 0.3) {
112                 data[i] = rand.nextGaussian() * 2 + 10;
113             } else {
114                 data[i] = rand.nextGaussian() * 1 + 2;
115             }
116         }
117
118         // fit GMM to data
119         int k = 2;
120         GaussianMixtureModel gmm = new GaussianMixtureModel(k, n);
121         gmm.fit(data);
122
123         // print cluster parameters
124         System.out.println("Cluster 1: mu=" + gmm.mu[0] + ", sigma=" + gmm.
        sigma[0] + ", pi=" + gmm.pi[0]);
```

```java
125     System.out.println("Cluster 2: mu=" + gmm.mu[1] + ", sigma=" + gmm.
        sigma[1] + ", pi=" + gmm.pi[1]);
126
127     // predict labels for new data points
128     System.out.println("Predicted labels:");
129     for (double x : new double[] {0.0, 2.0, 5.0, 8.0, 10.0}) {
130         System.out.println(x + ": " + gmm.predict(x));
131     }
132   }
133 }
```

This implementation uses the Expectation-Maximization algorithm to estimate the cluster parameters. The 'fit' method initializes the cluster parameters randomly, then iteratively updates them using the E-step and M-step until convergence. The 'predict' method assigns a data point to the cluster with the highest probability.

To use this implementation, you can create a new 'GaussianMixtureModel' object with the desired number of clusters 'k' and number of data points 'n', then call the 'fit' method with an array of data points. After fitting the model, you can access the cluster parameters using the 'mu', 'sigma', and 'pi' arrays. To predict labels for new data points, you can call the 'predict' method with a single data point.

§ 5   Maximum Likelihood Estimation

Here's an example implementation of Maximum Likelihood Estimation in C++ for a simple linear regression model:

```cpp
1  #include <iostream>
2  #include <vector>
3  #include <cmath>
4
5  using namespace std;
6
7  // Define the linear regression model
8  double linear_regression(double x, double slope, double intercept) {
9      return slope * x + intercept;
10 }
11
12 // Define the likelihood function
13 double likelihood(vector<double> x, vector<double> y, double slope,
       double intercept) {
14     double log_likelihood = 0;
15     for (int i = 0; i < x.size(); i++) {
16         double mu = linear_regression(x[i], slope, intercept);
17         double sigma = 1; // assume unit variance
18         log_likelihood += log(1 / (sqrt(2 * M_PI) * sigma)) - pow((y[i] -
       mu), 2) / (2 * pow(sigma, 2));
19     }
20     return log_likelihood;
21 }
```

```
22
23 // Define the gradient of the likelihood function with respect to slope
24 double gradient_slope(vector<double> x, vector<double> y, double slope,
       double intercept) {
25     double gradient = 0;
26     for (int i = 0; i < x.size(); i++) {
27         double mu = linear_regression(x[i], slope, intercept);
28         gradient += (y[i] - mu) * x[i];
29     }
30     return gradient;
31 }
32
33 // Define the gradient of the likelihood function with respect to
       intercept
34 double gradient_intercept(vector<double> x, vector<double> y, double
       slope, double intercept) {
35     double gradient = 0;
36     for (int i = 0; i < x.size(); i++) {
37         double mu = linear_regression(x[i], slope, intercept);
38         gradient += (y[i] - mu);
39     }
40     return gradient;
41 }
42
43 // Perform Maximum Likelihood Estimation
44 void maximum_likelihood(vector<double> x, vector<double> y, double& slope
       , double& intercept, double learning_rate, int num_iterations) {
45     for (int i = 0; i < num_iterations; i++) {
46         double gradient_slope_val = gradient_slope(x, y, slope, intercept
       );
47         double gradient_intercept_val = gradient_intercept(x, y, slope,
       intercept);
48         slope += learning_rate * gradient_slope_val;
49         intercept += learning_rate * gradient_intercept_val;
50         double log_likelihood = likelihood(x, y, slope, intercept);
51         cout << "Iteration " << i + 1 << ": slope=" << slope << ",
       intercept=" << intercept << ", log likelihood=" << log_likelihood <<
       endl;
52     }
53 }
54
55 int main() {
56     // Generate data
57     vector<double> x = {1, 2, 3, 4, 5};
58     vector<double> y = {3.2, 4.1, 5.3, 6.4, 7.5};
59
60     // Initialize parameters
61     double slope = 0;
62     double intercept = 0;
63
64     // Set learning rate and number of iterations
```

```
65    double learning_rate = 0.01;
66    int num_iterations = 1000;
67
68    // Perform Maximum Likelihood Estimation
69    maximum_likelihood(x, y, slope, intercept, learning_rate,
      num_iterations);
70
71    // Print results
72    cout << "Final Parameters: slope=" << slope << ", intercept=" <<
      intercept << endl;
73
74    return 0;
75 }
```

In this implementation, we define the linear regression model, the likelihood function, and the gradients of the likelihood function with respect to the model parameters (slope and intercept). We then perform Maximum Likelihood Estimation using gradient ascent, updating the model parameters iteratively until convergence.

§ 6   Expectation-Maximization Algorithm

Here's an example implementation of the Expectation-Maximization (EM) Algorithm in Fortran for a simple Gaussian Mixture Model:

```
1  program em_algorithm
2     implicit none
3
4     integer, parameter :: num_data_points = 100 ! number of data points
5     integer, parameter :: num_clusters = 2 ! number of clusters
6     integer :: i, j, k
7     real, parameter :: pi = 3.14159265358979323846
8     real, parameter :: tolerance = 1e-6 ! tolerance for convergence
9     real, parameter :: epsilon = 1e-6 ! small number to avoid division by
       zero
10
11    real, dimension(num_data_points) :: x ! data points
12    real, dimension(num_clusters) :: pi_k ! mixing coefficients for each
       cluster
13    real, dimension(num_clusters) :: mu_k ! mean for each cluster
14    real, dimension(num_clusters) :: sigma_k ! standard deviation for
       each cluster
15    real, dimension(num_data_points,num_clusters) :: gamma_ij !
       responsibility for each data point and cluster
16
17    ! initialize data points
18    do i = 1, num_data_points
19        x(i) = 10 * (rand() - 0.5)
20    end do
21
22    ! initialize parameters
```

```fortran
   do k = 1, num_clusters
       pi_k(k) = 1 / real(num_clusters)
       mu_k(k) = 10 * (rand() - 0.5)
       sigma_k(k) = abs(10 * (rand() - 0.5))
   end do

   ! run EM algorithm
   do
       ! E-step: compute the responsibilities
       do i = 1, num_data_points
           do k = 1, num_clusters
               gamma_ij(i,k) = pi_k(k) * exp(-0.5 * ((x(i) - mu_k(k)) / &
   (sigma_k(k) + epsilon))**2) / &
                               ((2 * pi) * (sigma_k(k) + epsilon))
           end do
           gamma_ij(i,:) = gamma_ij(i,:) / sum(gamma_ij(i,:))
       end do

       ! M-step: update the parameters
       do k = 1, num_clusters
           pi_k(k) = sum(gamma_ij(:,k)) / real(num_data_points)
           mu_k(k) = dot_product(gamma_ij(:,k), x) / sum(gamma_ij(:,k))
           sigma_k(k) = sqrt(dot_product(gamma_ij(:,k), (x - mu_k(k)) &
   **2) / sum(gamma_ij(:,k)))
       end do

       ! check for convergence
       if (max(abs(gamma_ij - gamma_ij_old)) < tolerance) exit
       gamma_ij_old = gamma_ij
   end do

   ! print the results
   write(*,*) 'Mixing Coefficients:'
   do k = 1, num_clusters
       write(*,'(F8.6)') pi_k(k)
   end do
   write(*,*)

   write(*,*) 'Means:'
   do k = 1, num_clusters
       write(*,'(F8.6)') mu_k(k)
   end do
   write(*,*)

   write(*,*) 'Standard Deviations:'
   do k = 1, num_clusters
       write(*,'(F8.6)') sigma_k(k)
   end do
end program em_algorithm
```

In this implementation, we first generate some random data points. We then initialize the parameters of the Gaussian Mixture Model (the mixing coefficients, means, and standard deviations of the clusters).

§ 7   Naive Bayes Classifier

Here's an example implementation of a Naive Bayes Classifier in C++ for binary classification:

```cpp
#include <iostream>
#include <vector>
#include <cmath>

using namespace std;

// calculate the probability density function of a normal distribution
double normal_pdf(double x, double mean, double stddev) {
    return exp(-(x - mean) * (x - mean) / (2 * stddev * stddev)) / (sqrt
    (2 * M_PI) * stddev);
}

// train the Naive Bayes Classifier
void train_naive_bayes_classifier(const vector<vector<double>>& X_train,
    const vector<int>& y_train, double& prior_0, double& prior_1, vector<
    double>& means_0, vector<double>& means_1, vector<double>& stddevs_0,
     vector<double>& stddevs_1) {
    int num_samples = X_train.size();
    int num_features = X_train[0].size();
    int num_samples_0 = 0;
    int num_samples_1 = 0;
    double sum_0, sum_1;

    // calculate the priors and means and standard deviations for each
    feature
    for (int i = 0; i < num_features; ++i) {
        sum_0 = 0;
        sum_1 = 0;
        for (int j = 0; j < num_samples; ++j) {
            if (y_train[j] == 0) {
                sum_0 += X_train[j][i];
                ++num_samples_0;
            }
            else {
                sum_1 += X_train[j][i];
                ++num_samples_1;
            }
        }
        means_0[i] = sum_0 / num_samples_0;
        means_1[i] = sum_1 / num_samples_1;

        sum_0 = 0;
        sum_1 = 0;
```

```
39      for (int j = 0; j < num_samples; ++j) {
40          if (y_train[j] == 0) {
41              sum_0 += (X_train[j][i] - means_0[i]) * (X_train[j][i] -
    means_0[i]);
42          }
43          else {
44              sum_1 += (X_train[j][i] - means_1[i]) * (X_train[j][i] -
    means_1[i]);
45          }
46      }
47      stddevs_0[i] = sqrt(sum_0 / num_samples_0);
48      stddevs_1[i] = sqrt(sum_1 / num_samples_1);
49   }

50
51   prior_0 = num_samples_0 / double(num_samples);
52   prior_1 = num_samples_1 / double(num_samples);
53 }
54
55 // predict the class of a new sample using the Naive Bayes Classifier
56 int predict_naive_bayes_classifier(const vector<double>& X, const double
     prior_0, const double prior_1, const vector<double>& means_0, const
     vector<double>& means_1, const vector<double>& stddevs_0, const
     vector<double>& stddevs_1) {
57   int num_features = X.size();
58   double p_0 = log(prior_0);
59   double p_1 = log(prior_1);
60
61   for (int i = 0; i < num_features; ++i) {
62       p_0 += log(normal_pdf(X[i], means_0[i], stddevs_0[i]));
63       p_1 += log(normal_pdf(X[i], means_1[i], stddevs_1[i]));
64   }
65
66   if (p_0 > p_1) {
67       return 0;
68   }
69   else {
70       return 1;
71   }
72 }
73 int main() {
74   // training data
75   vector<vector<double>> X_train = {{1, 2}, {2, 3}, {3, 3}, {2, 1}, {3,
     2}, {1, 3}};
76   vector<int> y_train = {0, 0, 0, 1, 1, 1};
77   // test data
78   vector<vector<double>> X_test = {{1, 1}, {2, 2}, {3, 1}};
79
80   // prior probabilities and parameters for each feature
81   double prior_0, prior_1;
82   vector<double> means_0(X_train[0].size()), means_1(X_train[0].size())
     ;
```

```
83    vector<double> stddevs_0(X_train[0].size()), stddevs_1(X_train[0].
      size());
84
85    // train the Naive Bayes Classifier
86    train_naive_bayes_classifier(X_train, y_train, prior_0, prior_1,
      means_0, means_1, stddevs_0, stddevs_1);
87
88    // predict the class of each test sample using the Naive Bayes
      Classifier
89    for (const auto& X : X_test) {
90        int y_pred = predict_naive_bayes_classifier(X, prior_0, prior_1,
      means_0, means_1, stddevs_0, stddevs_1);
91        cout << "Predicted class: " << y_pred << endl;
92    }
93
94    return 0;
95 }
```

In this implementation, the 'normal_pdf()' function calculates the probability density function of a normal distribution, given the mean and standard deviation. The train_naive_bayes _classifier() function trains the Naive Bayes Classifier on the training data, using maximum likelihood estimation to calculate the prior probabilities and mean and standard deviation for each feature. The 'predict_naive_bayes_classifier()' function predicts the class of a new sample, given the prior probabilities and mean and standard deviation for each feature.

In the 'main()' function, we train the Naive Bayes Classifier on the training data and then predict the class of each test sample using the trained classifier.

§ 8   Decision Tree

Here's an example implementation of the Decision Trees algorithm in Java:

```
1  import java.util.*;
2
3  public class DecisionTree {
4      private static class Node {
5          int attribute;
6          int label;
7          List<Node> children;
8
9          Node(int attr) {
10             attribute = attr;
11             children = new ArrayList<>();
12         }
13     }
14
15     private static Node buildDecisionTree(List<List<Integer>> X, List<
       Integer> y, List<Integer> attrs) {
16         // Check for stopping conditions
17         if (attrs.size() == 0) {
```

```java
            Node leaf = new Node(-1);
            leaf.label = majorityVote(y);
            return leaf;
        }
        if (sameLabel(y)) {
            Node leaf = new Node(-1);
            leaf.label = y.get(0);
            return leaf;
        }

        // Find best attribute to split on
        int bestAttr = findBestSplit(X, y, attrs);
        List<List<Integer>>[] subsets = splitData(X, y, bestAttr);

        // Create new node with best attribute
        Node node = new Node(bestAttr);

        // Recursively build decision tree for each subset
        for (int i = 0; i < subsets.length; i++) {
            if (subsets[i].size() == 0) {
                Node leaf = new Node(-1);
                leaf.label = majorityVote(y);
                node.children.add(leaf);
            } else {
                List<Integer> newX = new ArrayList<>();
                List<Integer> newY = new ArrayList<>();
                for (int j = 0; j < subsets[i].size(); j++) {
                    newX.add(subsets[i].get(j).get(0));
                    newY.add(subsets[i].get(j).get(1));
                }
                List<Integer> newAttrs = new ArrayList<>(attrs);
                newAttrs.remove(Integer.valueOf(bestAttr));
                node.children.add(buildDecisionTree(newX, newY, newAttrs)
);
            }
        }

        return node;
    }

    private static boolean sameLabel(List<Integer> y) {
        int label = y.get(0);
        for (int i = 1; i < y.size(); i++) {
            if (y.get(i) != label) {
                return false;
            }
        }
        return true;
    }

    private static int majorityVote(List<Integer> y) {
```

```java
        Map<Integer, Integer> freq = new HashMap<>();
        for (int i = 0; i < y.size(); i++) {
            int label = y.get(i);
            freq.put(label, freq.getOrDefault(label, 0) + 1);
        }
        int maxFreq = -1;
        int maxLabel = -1;
        for (int label : freq.keySet()) {
            int count = freq.get(label);
            if (count > maxFreq) {
                maxFreq = count;
                maxLabel = label;
            }
        }
        return maxLabel;
    }

    private static int findBestSplit(List<List<Integer>> X, List<Integer>
    y, List<Integer> attrs) {
        int bestAttr = -1;
        double bestInfoGain = -1.0;
        for (int attr : attrs) {
            double infoGain = calculateInfoGain(X, y, attr);
            if (infoGain > bestInfoGain) {
                bestInfoGain = infoGain;
                bestAttr = attr;
            }
        }
        return bestAttr;
    }

    private static double calculateInfoGain(List<List<Integer>> X, List<
    Integer> y, int attr) {
        double entropy = calculateEntropy(y);
        List<List<Integer>>[] subsets = splitData(X, y, attr);
        double subsetEntropy = 0.0;
    for (int i = 0; i < subsets.length; i++) {
        if (subsets[i].size() > 0) {
            double weight = (double) subsets[i].size() / (double) X.size
    ();
            subsetEntropy += weight * calculateEntropy(getLabels(subsets[
    i]));
        }
    }
    return entropy - subsetEntropy;
}

private static double calculateEntropy(List<Integer> y) {
    Map<Integer, Integer> freq = new HashMap<>();
    for (int i = 0; i < y.size(); i++) {
        int label = y.get(i);
```

```
115         freq.put(label, freq.getOrDefault(label, 0) + 1);
116     }
117     double entropy = 0.0;
118     for (int label : freq.keySet()) {
119         double p = (double) freq.get(label) / (double) y.size();
120         entropy -= p * Math.log(p) / Math.log(2);
121     }
122     return entropy;
123 }
124
125 private static List<List<Integer>>[] splitData(List<List<Integer>> X,
        List<Integer> y, int attr) {
126     List<List<Integer>>[] subsets = new List[2];
127     subsets[0] = new ArrayList<>();
128     subsets[1] = new ArrayList<>();
129     for (int i = 0; i < X.size(); i++) {
130         if (X.get(i).get(attr) == 0) {
131             subsets[0].add(Arrays.asList(X.get(i).get(attr), y.get(i)));
132         } else {
133             subsets[1].add(Arrays.asList(X.get(i).get(attr), y.get(i)));
134         }
135     }
136     return subsets;
137 }
138
139 private static List<Integer> getLabels(List<List<Integer>>[] subsets) {
140     List<Integer> labels = new ArrayList<>();
141     for (int i = 0; i < subsets.length; i++) {
142         for (int j = 0; j < subsets[i].size(); j++) {
143             labels.add(subsets[i].get(j).get(1));
144         }
145     }
146     return labels;
147 }
148
149 private static int predict(Node root, List<Integer> example) {
150     while (root.attribute != -1) {
151         int attr = root.attribute;
152         root = root.children.get(example.get(attr));
153     }
154     return root.label;
155 }
156
157 public static void main(String[] args) {
158     List<List<Integer>> X = new ArrayList<>();
159     List<Integer> y = new ArrayList<>();
160
161     // Add training examples
162     X.add(Arrays.asList(0, 1, 0));
163     X.add(Arrays.asList(1, 0, 1));
164     X.add(Arrays.asList(1, 1, 1));
```

```
165        X.add(Arrays.asList(0, 0, 1));
166        X.add(Arrays.asList(1, 1, 0));
167        X.add(Arrays.asList(0, 1, 1));
168        y.add(0);
169        y.add(1);
170        y.add(1);
171        y.add(1);
172        y.add(0);
173        y.add(1);
174
175        List<Integer> attrs = new ArrayList<>();
176        attrs.add(0);
177        attrs.add(1);
178        attrs.add(2);
179
180        Node root = buildDecisionTree(X, y, attrs);
181
182        // Predict class of new example
183        List<Integer> example = Arrays.asList(1, 0, 0);
184        int label = predict(root, example);
185        System.out.println("Predicted class: " + label);
186    }
187 }
```

This code defines a 'Node' class to represent the nodes in the decision tree, with an 'attribute' field indicating which attribute to split on at that node, a 'label' field indicating the predicted class at that node (if it is a leaf node), and a children field containing a list of child nodes. The buildDecisionTree function takes in the training data X and their labels y, as well as a list of attributes attrs to consider for splitting. It recursively builds the decision tree by choosing the attribute that maximizes the information gain at each node, until all examples have the same label or no attributes are left to split on.

The calculateInformationGain function calculates the information gain for a given attribute, using the formula: entropy(parent) - sum(weight(subset) * entropy(subset)) for all possible subsets created by splitting on the attribute. The calculateEntropy function calculates the entropy of a set of labels, using the formula: - sum(p * log2(p)) for all possible labels, where p is the proportion of examples with that label.

The splitData function splits the data into two subsets based on the given attribute, and the getLabels function extracts the labels from a list of subsets. Finally, the predict function traverses the decision tree to predict the class of a new example.

The main function creates a small example dataset and trains a decision tree on it. It then predicts the class of a new example and prints the result.

§ 9   Logistic Regression

Here is the implementation we make for this in fortran:

```
1 program logistic_regression
```

```fortran
implicit none

integer, parameter :: n_features = 2
integer, parameter :: n_examples = 100
real, parameter :: learning_rate = 0.01
integer, parameter :: n_iterations = 1000

real :: X(n_features, n_examples)
real :: y(n_examples)
real :: w(n_features)
real :: b
integer :: i, j, k
real :: z, a, dw(n_features), db

! Generate example data
call random_seed()
do i = 1, n_examples
  X(:,i) = [1.0, random_uniform()]   ! Add bias term
  y(i) = (X(2,i) > 0.5)              ! Classify based on second feature
end do

! Initialize parameters
w = 0.1 * random_number() - 0.05
b = 0.1 * random_number() - 0.05

! Train logistic regression model
do i = 1, n_iterations
  dw = 0.0
  db = 0.0
  do j = 1, n_examples
    z = dot_product(w, X(:,j)) + b
    a = 1.0 / (1.0 + exp(-z))
    dw = dw + (a - y(j)) * X(:,j)
    db = db + (a - y(j))
  end do
  dw = dw / n_examples
  db = db / n_examples
  w = w - learning_rate * dw
  b = b - learning_rate * db
end do

! Print parameters
print *, "w = ", w
print *, "b = ", b

end program logistic_regression
```

This implementation uses a simple gradient descent algorithm to optimize the logistic regression model. The X matrix contains the input features, with each row corresponding to a feature and each column corresponding to an example. The y vector contains the corresponding labels, with a value of 0 or 1 indicating the class of each example. The w vector contains the weights for each feature, and the b scalar contains the bias term.

The dot_product function computes the dot product of two vectors, and the exp function computes the exponential function. The learning_rate parameter controls the step size in the gradient descent algorithm, and the n_iterations parameter controls the number of iterations to run.

The algorithm computes the gradient of the logistic loss function with respect to the weights and bias, and updates them using the gradient descent rule. At the end of training, the parameters w and b represent the learned logistic regression model.

§ 10   Hidden Markov Model

Here is the implementation of Hidden Markov Model in ada:

```ada
with Ada.Text_IO; use Ada.Text_IO;

procedure HMM is
  -- Define the model parameters
  N : constant := 2; -- Number of hidden states
  M : constant := 3; -- Number of observable symbols
  A : array (1..N, 1..N) of Float := ((0.7, 0.3), (0.3, 0.7)); --
    Transition matrix
  B : array (1..N, 1..M) of Float := ((0.1, 0.4, 0.5), (0.7, 0.2, 0.1));
    -- Emission matrix
  pi : array (1..N) of Float := (0.6, 0.4); -- Initial state distribution

  -- Define the observations
  T : constant := 4; -- Length of the observation sequence
  O : array (1..T) of Integer := (1, 3, 2, 3); -- Observation sequence

  -- Define the alpha and beta matrices
  alpha : array (1..T, 1..N) of Float;
  beta : array (1..T, 1..N) of Float;

  -- Compute the forward probabilities using the alpha matrix
  procedure Forward is
  begin
    -- Initialize the alpha matrix
    for i in 1..N loop
      alpha(1, i) := pi(i) * B(i, O(1));
    end loop;

    -- Compute the alpha matrix recursively
    for t in 2..T loop
      for j in 1..N loop
        alpha(t, j) := 0.0;
        for i in 1..N loop
          alpha(t, j) := alpha(t, j) + alpha(t-1, i) * A(i, j);
        end loop;
```

```
           alpha(t, j) := alpha(t, j) * B(j, O(t));
         end loop;
       end loop;
   end Forward;

   -- Compute the backward probabilities using the beta matrix
   procedure Backward is
   begin
       -- Initialize the beta matrix
       for i in 1..N loop
         beta(T, i) := 1.0;
       end loop;

       -- Compute the beta matrix recursively
       for t in T-1..1 loop
         for i in 1..N loop
           beta(t, i) := 0.0;
           for j in 1..N loop
             beta(t, i) := beta(t, i) + A(i, j) * B(j, O(t+1)) * beta(t+1, j
   );
           end loop;
         end loop;
       end loop;
   end Backward;

   -- Compute the probability of the observation sequence using the alpha
    matrix
   function Observation_Probability return Float is
     p : Float := 0.0;
   begin
     for i in 1..N loop
       p := p + alpha(T, i);
     end loop;
     return p;
   end Observation_Probability;

begin
   -- Compute the forward probabilities using the alpha matrix
   Forward;

   -- Compute the backward probabilities using the beta matrix
   Backward;

   -- Compute the probability of the observation sequence using the alpha
    matrix
   Put_Line("Observation probability: " & Float'Image(
     Observation_Probability));

   -- Compute the state probabilities using the alpha and beta matrices
   for t in 1..T loop
   Put_Line("State probabilities at time " & Integer'Image(t));
```

```ada
81    for i in 1..N loop
82       Put("State " & Integer'Image(i) & ": ");
83       Put(Float'Image(alpha(t, i) * beta(t, i) / Observation_Probability) &
         ", ");
84    end loop;
85   New_Line;
86 end loop;
87 end HMM;
```

This code defines a simple HMM with two hidden states and three observable symbols, and computes the probability of an observation sequence using the forward algorithm, as well as the state probabilities at each time step using the alpha and beta matrices. Note that this is just a simple example, and in practice, HMMs can be much more complex and may require more efficient algorithms and data structures.

§ 11   K-Nearest Neighbors

Here is an implementation for K-Nearest Neighbors in C:

```c
1  #include <stdio.h>
2  #include <stdlib.h>
3  #include <math.h>
4
5  #define K 3
6  #define NUM_FEATURES 2
7  #define NUM_SAMPLES 6
8
9  typedef struct {
10     float features[NUM_FEATURES];
11     int label;
12 } Sample;
13
14 float euclidean_distance(float *x1, float *x2) {
15     float distance = 0.0;
16     for (int i = 0; i < NUM_FEATURES; i++) {
17         distance += pow(x1[i] - x2[i], 2);
18     }
19     return sqrt(distance);
20 }
21
22 int predict(Sample *samples, float *test, int num_samples) {
23     float distances[num_samples];
24     for (int i = 0; i < num_samples; i++) {
25         distances[i] = euclidean_distance(samples[i].features, test);
26     }
27     int indices[num_samples];
28     for (int i = 0; i < num_samples; i++) {
29         indices[i] = i;
30     }
31     for (int i = 0; i < num_samples - 1; i++) {
```

```
32          for (int j = i + 1; j < num_samples; j++) {
33              if (distances[i] > distances[j]) {
34                  float temp_distance = distances[i];
35                  int temp_index = indices[i];
36                  distances[i] = distances[j];
37                  indices[i] = indices[j];
38                  distances[j] = temp_distance;
39                  indices[j] = temp_index;
40              }
41          }
42      }
43      int class_count[NUM_SAMPLES] = {0};
44      for (int i = 0; i < K; i++) {
45          int index = indices[i];
46          int label = samples[index].label;
47          class_count[label]++;
48      }
49      int max_count = 0;
50      int max_index = -1;
51      for (int i = 0; i < NUM_SAMPLES; i++) {
52          if (class_count[i] > max_count) {
53              max_count = class_count[i];
54              max_index = i;
55          }
56      }
57      return max_index;
58  }
59
60  int main() {
61      Sample samples[NUM_SAMPLES] = {
62          {{1.0, 1.1}, 0},
63          {{1.0, 1.0}, 0},
64          {{0.0, 0.0}, 1},
65          {{0.0, 0.1}, 1},
66          {{0.0, 0.2}, 1},
67          {{0.1, 0.1}, 1},
68      };
69      float test[NUM_FEATURES] = {0.1, 0.2};
70      int prediction = predict(samples, test, NUM_SAMPLES);
71      printf("Predicted class: %d\n", prediction);
72      return 0;
73  }
```

This implementation defines a Sample struct that stores the features and label of a sample, and defines a predict function that takes an array of samples, a test sample, and the number of samples as input, and returns the predicted label of the test sample using the K-Nearest Neighbors algorithm. The euclidean_distance function is used to compute the Euclidean distance between two feature vectors, and the predicted label is computed by counting the labels of the K nearest neighbors to the test sample and returning the most common label. The example main function defines a small dataset and a test sample, and prints the predicted label of the test sample.

§ 12   Random Forests

Here is an example implementation of Random Forests algorithm in Fortran:

```fortran
program random_forest

implicit none

! Parameters
integer, parameter :: num_features = 4
integer, parameter :: num_trees = 3
integer, parameter :: max_depth = 3
integer, parameter :: num_samples = 10
integer, parameter :: num_classes = 2
real, parameter :: min_sample_split = 2.0
real, parameter :: min_impurity_decrease = 0.0
real, parameter :: eps = 1e-12
integer :: num_selected_features
integer, parameter :: num_random_features = 2

! Types
type Sample
    real :: features(num_features)
    integer :: label
end type Sample

type Node
    integer :: feature_index
    real :: threshold
    type(Node), pointer :: left => null()
    type(Node), pointer :: right => null()
end type Node

type Tree
    type(Node), pointer :: root => null()
end type Tree

type Forest
    type(Tree), dimension(num_trees) :: trees
end type Forest

! Variables
integer :: i, j, k, m, n
real, dimension(num_samples, num_features) :: features
integer, dimension(num_samples) :: labels
type(Sample), dimension(num_samples) :: samples
type(Forest) :: forest
real, dimension(num_random_features) :: selected_features
```

```fortran
real, dimension(num_samples) :: weights
real :: max_weight
real :: impurity
integer :: best_feature
real :: best_threshold
real :: best_impurity
type(Node), pointer :: root => null()

! Random number generator
call random_seed()
call random_seed(size = n)
do i = 1, 10 * n
    call random_number()
end do

! Generate dataset
do i = 1, num_samples
    do j = 1, num_features
        call random_number(features(i,j))
        samples(i)%features(j) = features(i,j)
    end do
    if (features(i,1) > 0.5) then
        samples(i)%label = 1
    else
        samples(i)%label = 0
    end if
end do

! Train random forest
do n = 1, num_trees
    ! Select random features
    do i = 1, num_random_features
        num_selected_features = 0
        do j = 1, num_features
            if (selected_features(i) == j) then
                num_selected_features = num_selected_features + 1
            end if
        end do
        do while (num_selected_features == i - 1)
            call random_number(selected_features(i))
            selected_features(i) = 1 + floor(selected_features(i) * num_features)
            num_selected_features = 0
            do j = 1, num_features
                if (selected_features(i) == j) then
                    num_selected_features = num_selected_features + 1
                end if
            end do
        end do
    end do
    ! Generate bootstrap sample
```

```fortran
      do i = 1, num_samples
          call random_number(weights(i))
      end do
      max_weight = maxval(weights)
      do i = 1, num_samples
          weights(i) = weights(i) / max_weight
      end do
      do i = 1, num_samples
          call random_number(j)
          j = 1 + floor(j * num_samples)
          features(i,:) = samples(j)%features
          labels(i) = samples(j)%label
      end do
      ! Train decision tree
      forest%trees(n)%root => build_tree(features, labels, weights, &
      selected_features, max_depth)

end do

contains

function build_tree(features, labels, weights, selected_features, depth) &
    result(node)

    ! Local variables
    integer :: i, j, k
    real, dimension(size(features,2)) :: thresholds
    real :: impurity, best_threshold
    integer :: best_feature
    real, dimension(size(labels)) :: left_labels, right_labels
    real, dimension(size(weights)) :: left_weights, right_weights
    real :: left_weight, right_weight
    type(Node), pointer :: left => null()
    type(Node), pointer :: right => null()

    ! Initialize node
    allocate(node)
    node%feature_index = 0
    node%threshold = 0.0
    node%left => null()
    node%right => null()

    ! Check if leaf node
    if (depth == 0 .or. size(labels) < min_sample_split) then
        node%feature_index = -1
        node%threshold = most_frequent_label(labels, weights)
        return
    end if

    ! Calculate impurity for each feature
    impurity = calculate_impurity(labels, weights)
```

```fortran
do i = 1, size(selected_features)
    if (selected_features(i) == 0) then
        cycle
    end if
    ! Calculate thresholds
    thresholds = calculate_thresholds(features(:,selected_features(i)), weights)
    do j = 1, size(thresholds)
        ! Split samples
        split_samples(features, labels, weights, selected_features(i), thresholds(j), &
            left_labels, right_labels, left_weights, right_weights, left_weight, right_weight)
        ! Calculate impurity decrease
        if (size(left_labels) >= min_sample_split .and. size(right_labels) >= min_sample_split) then
            if (impurity - calculate_weighted_impurity(left_labels, right_labels, left_weights, right_weights) &
                > best_impurity) then
                best_feature = selected_features(i)
                best_threshold = thresholds(j)
                best_impurity = impurity - calculate_weighted_impurity(left_labels, right_labels, left_weights, right_weights)
                left_weight = left_weight
                right_weight = right_weight
            end if
        end if
    end do
end do

! Check if leaf node
if (best_feature == 0) then
    node%feature_index = -1
    node%threshold = most_frequent_label(labels, weights)
    return
end if

! Split samples
split_samples(features, labels, weights, best_feature, best_threshold, &
    left_labels, right_labels, left_weights, right_weights, left_weight, right_weight)

! Build left subtree
if (size(left_labels) > 0) then
    node%left => build_tree(features, left_labels, left_weights, selected_features, depth - 1)
else
    node%left => null()
end if
```

```fortran
      ! Build right subtree
      if (size(right_labels) > 0) then
          node%right => build_tree(features, right_labels, right_weights,
      selected_features, depth - 1)
      else
          node%right => null()
      end if

end function build_tree

function calculate_impurity(labels, weights) result(impurity)

      ! Local variables
      integer :: i, j
      real :: num_samples_left, num_samples_right
      real :: impurity_left, impurity_right
      real :: sum_weights, sum_weights_left, sum_weights_right

      ! Calculate impurity of current node
      sum_weights = sum(weights)
      impurity = 0.0
      do i = 1, size(unique_labels)
          j = index(labels, unique_labels(i))
          if (j > 0) then
              impurity = impurity + (weights(j) / sum_weights) * (1.0 - (
      weights(j) / sum_weights))
          end if
      end do

      ! Calculate impurity of left node
      num_samples_left = sum(weights * (labels <= threshold))
      if (num_samples_left > 0) then
          sum_weights_left = sum(weights * (labels <= threshold))
          impurity_left = 0.0
          do i = 1, size(unique_labels)
              j = index(labels * (labels <= threshold), unique_labels(i))
              if (j > 0) then
                  impurity_left = impurity_left + (weights(j) /
      sum_weights_left) * (1.0 - (weights(j) / sum_weights_left))
              end if
          end do
          impurity = impurity - (sum_weights_left / sum_weights) *
      impurity_left
      end if

      ! Calculate impurity of right node
      num_samples_right = sum(weights * (labels > threshold))
      if (num_samples_right > 0) then
          sum_weights_right = sum(weights * (labels > threshold))
          impurity_right = 0.0
```

```fortran
232         do i = 1, size(unique_labels)
233            j = index(labels * (labels > threshold), unique_labels(i))
234            if (j > 0) then
235               impurity_right = impurity_right + (weights(j) / &
      sum_weights_right) * (1.0 - (weights(j) / sum_weights_right))
236            end if
237         end do
238         impurity = impurity - (sum_weights_right / sum_weights) * &
      impurity_right
239      end if
240 end function calculate_impurity
241
242 function calculate_weighted_impurity(left_labels, right_labels, &
      left_weights, right_weights) result(impurity)
243    ! Local variables
244    integer :: i, j, k
245    real :: sum_weights, sum_weights_left, sum_weights_right
246    real :: impurity_left, impurity_right
247
248    ! Calculate impurity of left node
249    sum_weights_left = sum(left_weights)
250    impurity_left = 0.0
251    do i = 1, size(unique_labels)
252       j = index(left_labels, unique_labels(i))
253       if (j > 0) then
254          impurity_left = impurity_left + (left_weights(j) / &
      sum_weights_left) * (1.0 - (left_weights(j) / sum_weights_left))
255       end if
256    end do
257
258    ! Calculate impurity of right node
259    sum_weights_right = sum(right_weights)
260    impurity_right = 0.0
261    do i = 1, size(unique_labels)
262       j = index(right_labels, unique_labels(i))
263       if (j > 0) then
264          impurity_right = impurity_right + (right_weights(j) / &
      sum_weights_right) * (1.0 - (right_weights(j) / sum_weights_right))
265       end if
266    end do
267
268     ! Calculate weighted impurity
269     sum_weights = sum(left_weights) + sum(right_weights)
270     impurity = (sum(left_weights) / sum_weights) * impurity_left + (sum( &
      right_weights) / sum_weights) * impurity_right
271    ! Calculate weighted impurity
272    sum_weights = sum(left_weights) + sum(right_weights)
273    impurity = (sum(left_weights) / sum_weights) * impurity_left + (sum( &
      right_weights) / sum_weights) * impurity_right
274
275 end function calculate_weighted_impurity
```

```fortran
276
277 function most_frequent_label(labels, weights) result(label)
278 ! Local variables
279    integer :: i, j
280    real :: max_count, count
281    integer :: label_index
282
283    ! Count labels
284    max_count = 0.0
285    do i = 1, size(labels)
286        count = 0.0
287        do j = 1, size(labels)
288            if (labels(i) == labels(j)) then
289                count = count + weights(j)
290            end if
291        end do
292        if (count > max_count) then
293            max_count = count
294            label_index = i
295        end if
296    end do
297
298    ! Return most frequent label
299    label = labels(label_index)
300 end function most_frequent_label
301
302 end module DecisionTree
303
304 end program rabdom_forests
```

Chapter 4

Optimization Theory

§ 1   Gradient Descent

Gradient Descent is an optimization algorithm used to minimize the cost function of a machine learning model. The basic idea of Gradient Descent is to update the parameters of the model iteratively in the direction of the negative gradient of the cost function, until the cost function is minimized.

Here's an implementation of Gradient Descent in C++:

```cpp
#include <iostream>
#include <vector>
#include <cmath>

using namespace std;

// Define the cost function
double cost_function(vector<double> X, vector<double> y, double m, double
    b) {
    double total_error = 0.0;
    int n = X.size();
    for (int i = 0; i < n; i++) {
        double x = X[i];
        double actual_y = y[i];
        double predicted_y = (m * x) + b;
        double error = actual_y - predicted_y;
        total_error += pow(error, 2);
    }
    return total_error / double(n);
}

// Define the gradient descent function
void gradient_descent(vector<double> X, vector<double> y, double &m,
    double &b, double alpha, int iterations) {
    int n = X.size();
    for (int i = 0; i < iterations; i++) {
        double gradient_m = 0.0;
```

```cpp
        double gradient_b = 0.0;
        for (int j = 0; j < n; j++) {
            double x = X[j];
            double actual_y = y[j];
            double predicted_y = (m * x) + b;
            double error = actual_y - predicted_y;
            gradient_m += (2.0 / double(n)) * (-x) * error;
            gradient_b += (2.0 / double(n)) * (-1) * error;
        }
        m = m - (alpha * gradient_m);
        b = b - (alpha * gradient_b);
    }
}

int main() {
    // Define the data
    vector<double> X = {1.0, 2.0, 3.0, 4.0, 5.0};
    vector<double> y = {2.0, 4.0, 6.0, 8.0, 10.0};

    // Define the initial parameters
    double m = 0.0;
    double b = 0.0;

    // Define the hyperparameters
    double alpha = 0.01;
    int iterations = 1000;

    // Run the gradient descent algorithm
    gradient_descent(X, y, m, b, alpha, iterations);

    // Print the final parameters
    cout << "Final Parameters: m = " << m << ", b = " << b << endl;

    // Calculate the final cost function
    double cost = cost_function(X, y, m, b);
    cout << "Final Cost: " << cost << endl;

    return 0;
}
```

In this implementation, the cost_function function takes in the input features (X), target variables (y), and the current values of the model parameters (m and b), and returns the mean squared error (MSE) of the predictions made by the model.

The gradient_descent function takes in the same input features and target variables, along with the current values of the model parameters (m and b), and two hyperparameters: the learning rate (alpha) and the number of iterations to run the algorithm (iterations). The function updates the values of m and b iteratively, using the gradient of the cost function with respect to each parameter, and the learning

§ 2   Newton Method

```cpp
#include <iostream>
#include <cmath>

using namespace std;

double f(double x) {
    // define the objective function
    return pow(x, 3) - x - 1;
}

double f_prime(double x) {
    // define the derivative of the objective function
    return 3 * pow(x, 2) - 1;
}

double newton_method(double x0, double eps) {
    double x = x0;
    double fx = f(x);
    double fpx = f_prime(x);

    while (abs(fx) > eps) {
        x = x - fx / fpx;  // update x using the Newton step
        fx = f(x);            // evaluate f(x) at the new x
        fpx = f_prime(x);  // evaluate f'(x) at the new x
    }

    return x;
}

int main() {
    double x0 = 1;        // initial guess for x
    double eps = 1e-6;    // tolerance for convergence
    double x = newton_method(x0, eps);

    cout << "The root of the function is: " << x << endl;

    return 0;
}
```

In this implementation, we define the objective function f(x) and its derivative f'(x) as separate functions. Then we define the newton_method function, which takes an initial guess x0 and a tolerance eps as input, and iteratively updates the value of x using the Newton step until the objective function is within eps of zero. Finally, we call newton_method with an initial guess of 1 and a tolerance of 1e-6, and print the resulting root.

Note that in practice, it's important to check that f_prime(x) is not equal to zero at any point during the iteration, since this would cause a division by zero error. We could also add a maximum number of iterations to prevent the algorithm from running indefinitely in case of convergence issues.

§ 3   Conjugate Gradient Method

Here is an implementation of Conjugate Gradient Method in fortran:

```fortran
program conjugate_gradient

implicit none

integer, parameter :: n = 3
real, parameter :: eps = 1e-6

integer :: i, j, k
real :: A(n,n), b(n), x(n), r(n), p(n), Ap(n)
real :: alpha, beta, rr, r_norm

! initialize A, b, and x
A = reshape([2.0, -1.0, 0.0, -1.0, 2.0, -1.0, 0.0, -1.0, 2.0], [n,n])
b = [1.0, 0.0, 1.0]
x = [0.0, 0.0, 0.0]

! initialize residual r and search direction p
r = b - matmul(A, x)
p = r

! iterate until convergence or maximum number of iterations is reached
do k = 1, n
    ! compute Ap = A*p
    Ap = matmul(A, p)

    ! compute alpha
    alpha = dot_product(r, r) / dot_product(p, Ap)

    ! update x and r
    x = x + alpha * p
    r = r - alpha * Ap

    ! check for convergence
    r_norm = sqrt(dot_product(r, r))
    if (r_norm < eps) then
        exit
    endif

    ! compute beta
    rr = dot_product(r, r)
    beta = rr / dot_product(p, Ap)

    ! update search direction p
    p = r + beta * p
end do

! print the solution
write(*, *) "The solution is:"
```

```
49  do i = 1, n
50      write(*, "(F8.4)") x(i)
51  end do
52
53  end program conjugate_gradient
```

In this implementation, we solve a system of linear equations Ax = b using the Conjugate Gradient Method, where A is a symmetric positive-definite matrix, b is the right-hand side vector, x is the solution vector, and eps is the tolerance for convergence.

We first define the problem parameters A, b, and x, and initialize the residual r and search direction p to be equal to b. We then iterate until convergence or a maximum number of iterations is reached, computing the matrix-vector product Ap, the step size alpha, and the search direction p at each iteration. We check for convergence by computing the norm of the residual r, and exit the loop if it is smaller than eps. Finally, we print the solution x.

Note that in practice, it's important to check that the matrix A is symmetric positive-definite to ensure that the algorithm converges correctly. We could also add a maximum number of iterations to prevent the algorithm from running indefinitely in case of convergence issues.